Christmas in Aspen

To: Jim

Jim Shirley

2010

Christmas in Aspen

By Jill Sheeley assisted by Diana Ryan   Illustrated by Ruth Stern

Courtney Press - Aspen, Colorado - 1981

First edition published in 1981 by Courtney Press, Aspen, Colorado.
Copyright©1981 by Jill Sheeley.
First Printing, 1981
Second Printing, 1982
Third Printing, 2003
ISBN 0-9609108-0-8
Printed in Korea

DEDICATION

This book is dedicated to the memory of
Hans Brucker
whose Christmas spirit lives in the hearts of us all.

Author's Note :
I published *Christmas In Aspen* in 1981. After two printings, I went on
to publish two cookbooks, five children's books and a coloring book.
After years of requests to reprint *Christmas In Aspen*, I finally
acquiesced. Please read this book knowing that it was written in 1980.
Much has changed since then, but I wanted to keep it an historical
treasure trove.

I dedicate this edition to the many dear and wonderful Aspenites
who grace these pages and who have passed away.

MAY PEACE AND LOVE BE WITH YOU THROUGHOUT THE
YEAR

Jill Sheeley

ACKNOWLEDGEMENTS

We would like to express our gratitude to the many people who helped us with this book:

All the families and individuals who contributed their time and their wonderful stories, songs, poetry and recipes.

Ruth—for her charming artwork and her many hours devoted to this book.

Ed, Patty, Jan, Dick, Jane and Pauli—for their patience in the tedious task of proofing.

Mary Eshbaugh Hayes—for her advice, knowledge and support.

Karen and Jane—for their many hours spent typing.

Don—for his marketing advice.

And to our parents for having faith in us.   ☐

TABLE OF CONTENTS

PART III — Recipes

PREFACE

$\mathcal{W}$hile hiking through the woods one crisp fall day, discussing ideas for Christmas gifts to make, we stumbled upon an idea which has now become a reality. Living in Aspen for many years has kindled warm feelings in us for our home and friends. This book is a tribute to a beautiful town and the people who have made Aspen what it is.

□

PART I

Family Stories

*A*spen is made up of remarkable people from all parts of the world. These people moved to the mountains in order to experience a life of adventure, culture, activities, peace, serenity and home.

Families grew, businesses prospered and dreams were realized.

Christmas in Aspen is a very special time of the year, as it is anywhere. The town is decorated and people are bustling around the streets shopping. Music is in the air and families are active, preparing for this festive and joyous holiday.

We have chosen several Aspen families who have shared with us their own unique celebration of Christmas. Interspersed among these stories are some favorite legends and songs. ◻

CHRISTMAS AT ANDERSON RANCH

as told to Linda Liddell by Hildur Anderson

I remember Dad would hitch the horses to the feed sled. My brothers would gather the sharpened axes and off they would go into the woods for the family's Christmas tree.

Busy in the kitchen, we would help Mother with decorations: popping corn, stringing cranberries, making paper rings, and dipping wax into candles for our new tree.

There was always a lot of preparation for this very special time of year, and everyone went about his own task with a joyful heart.

We all helped with the churning of the butter, making jam and grinding the wheat for Mother's famous coffee bread.

Then came the time for Father to slaughter a nice fat turkey. Mother would go out to the barnyard and do a little dance with the noisy birds, finally selecting the best one. It was Father's job to dress it out and all the kids pulled feathers until the bird was cleaned and ready to stuff and bake.

Christmas Eve was greeted with great anticipation. Our stockings were hung by the old wood stove, and bowls of rice with fresh cream and sugar were placed on the table for Christmas Eve dinner, a Swedish tradition that has stayed in our family.

Such excitement on Christmas Day —all six children rising with the first crow, ready to find their dreams wrapped in red and green paper.

There was always a new sled for someone, and you could always count on Mother's hand-knitted love woven into mittens and scarfs for each one of us. Dolls came from the big Sears catalogue along with the new .22 rifle for rabbit hunting.

On Christmas afternoon, we would gather around the old upright piano and sing carols with the neighbors who came by, while the candles glowed on the tree and the sound of the fire crackled to keep us warm.

The smells from the kitchen were heavenly: Mother's breads and fruit cakes cooling in the pie cabinet, all the wonderful things baking in the wood stove—sweet potatoes, turkey with bread stuffing and squash pie.

Our Christmas Day feast always began with fruit soup, a delightful combination of plums, raisins, rice, and tapioca served with homemade crackers.

The turkey arrived in great splendor on a large china platter decorated with cranberries and parsley. Dad carved and Mother dished onto our plates all her long hours and loving care in the kitchen.

Christmas on the ranch will always have special memories of a time when "just plain living" was a lot of very hard work; a time when our family was together, and what we shared in the good times and in the lean was our real gift to each other. *Merry Christmas!*

THE WIRTHS

Imagine spending Christmas on top of Aspen Mountain with a light snow falling. Imagine Santa delivering goodies to the children, and a close friend singing carols in German beside a candlelit tree. This fairy tale came true each year for the Wirths.

Upon the arrival of the Christmas season, Paul would step into his beartrap bindings on his wooden Army surplus skis and telemark into the forest in search of the perfect tree. He tells of the time that he cut down a tree, and after several attempts, hoisted it onto the single chairlift, which brought it to the top of the mountain! Their first tree at the Sundeck Restaurant was a living evergreen which they decorated outside. Upon awakening after one wintery night, they discovered their ornaments had blown away. From then on, you could find their tree inside with ornaments intact. From Switzerland came candle holders and the tradition of chocolate wrapped candies to hang on the tree.

Early in the fall, Paul's wife Hanna would do all her Christmas shopping, since they spent the entire winter season on top of the mountain. Having five inquisitive children—Anne Marie, Susan, Peter, Heidi and Paul Jr., great pains were taken to hide the gifts in limited space.

Their Christmas celebration would start at the close of the lifts on Christmas Eve. They dined on roast beef beside the fireplace. This was the only source of heat for the Sundeck at that time. After the meal, plays or skits were performed by the children. Santa arrived out of the snowy night to surprise the children and deliver small gifts from his bag. The delighted children then opened the gifts under the candle-lit tree. Their Christmas Eve was ended on a peaceful note with German carols sung by all.

Paul sums it up by reminiscing, "There's nothing like Christmas on top of a mountain!"

□

Tinsel

We found a lovely explanation for the origin of why Christmas trees are decorated with tinsel. Once upon a time, a mother of a very large family generously decorated the family's Christmas tree. One night, while everyone slept, spiders visited the tree and spun their beautiful webs from branch to branch. These incredible webs were blessed by the Christ Child, and transformed into shining silver.

□

THE MORSES

Anne Vitte Morse moved from Randers, Denmark, to Aspen in 1964. She met Terry here and they were married in 1967. They have three lovely children—Natasha, Sine and Hesse.

Anne Vitte loves Christmas and maintains many of her Scandinavian customs. She says, "I feel more Danish here than I did in Denmark."

She starts the first week of December by cleaning the house thoroughly. She makes a wreath for the door every year and decorates it with juniper berries and dried aspen flowers. The children get involved in the Christmas spirit and spend much time decorating their own rooms.

They celebrate St. Nick's Day on December 6th, and, being Aspen kids, they put out their Sorel boots. The children are delighted to find their boots filled with candy.

They also observe Advent. Anne Vitte tells us, "On the first Sunday in December, we start celebrating Advent. I make a wreath of greens and four white candles ... string it around with red ribbons and hang it from the kitchen ceiling. In the evening, we light the first candle, sing Danish Christmas songs, and give each child a little gift (mostly something they need like socks or mittens). We do this each of the four Sundays of Advent."

Their Christmas tree is decorated with all homemade ornaments and candles instead of electric lights. Anne Vitte brought all the candlestick holders over from Denmark.

"We surprise the children on Christmas Eve by opening our double doors and showing them the tree for the first time all lit up. We sing songs, exchange gifts and dance around the tree."

She and her family also celebrate, on December 13th, the Swedish Feast Day of St. Lucia. St. Lucia was a Sicilian maiden who suffered martyrdom in the year 304. Since she was noted for her generosity, giving food and drink to the poor, it is customary to perform such deeds on her day in memory of this maiden.

"The youngest of the daughters portrays St. Lucia and wears a wreath of greens and candles in her hair, and she and all the other children wind their way through the house at dawn, singing and taking their parents fresh saffron buns and tea on a tray lit with candles. The candles symbolize the keeping away of darkness of which people used to be so afraid."

In Denmark, everyone decorates the trees in front of their homes for the birds. Anne Vitte remembers, "They tie bunches of oats [that look like bells] to the trees with bright red ribbons. It's really so beautiful, and that way the birds can enjoy Christmas, too!"

□

Caroling Folklore

In the early Middle Ages, caroling, which at that time was portrayed by a group singing, holding hands and dancing in a circle, was thought to be paganistic both by the Church and by respectable Christian citizens.

There is an old folklore tale called "The Cursed Carollers of Kölbigk." It was told by a monk who claimed to be one of the only survivors of the miracle which supposedly happened in Saxony in about 1020.

Twelve carolers gathered at the church of St. Magnus in Kölbigk on Christmas Eve. The leader of the group was a fellow named Gerluus and he was accompanied by two maidens, Mersuind and Wibecyna. These three forcibly dragged the priest's daughter, Ava, in to the circle. They all then joined hands and danced in the churchyard.

As they danced in a circle, Gerluus sang the verses which told how one Bovo "rode into the woodlands leading the fair Mersuind" at which the rest of the group echoed the refrain, "Why do we stand here? Why don't we go too?" Upon hearing the carolers, the priest was obliged to ask them to cease their folly and come to services. When they flippantly refused, the righteous father became so angry that he invoked the wrath of the Lord upon them through the Saint Magnus. Immediately, the carolers discovered that they could not stop dancing or even break the circle no matter how hard they tried. For one whole year the weary dancers ironically were forced to clap and leap and sing, "Why do we stand here?" People from miles around came to see them. The Emperor Henry tried to have a shelter built above then, but each night it was mysteriously broken down. The following Christmas Eve, the curse was finally lifted and the fully repentant carolers went into the church where they fell asleep and awakened seventy-two hours later.

This is one of the earliest references to caroling. However, carols on Christmas Eve and other festive occasions were common in Western Europe long before 1020. Pagan round dances and carols became a popular form of entertainment in the Middle Ages.

The Church, being conscious of this popularity of caroling, decided something had to be done. This is where the philosophy of "If you can't beat them, join them" came into being. St. Francis of Assisi may not have originated the idea of sacred song in Italy and Europe in the thirteenth century, but he was mainly responsible for replacing "riotous carols" with more appropriate ones. His musical plan was to attach pious lyrics to tunes that had long been filled with messages worldly or worse. □

DECK THE HALLS WITH BOUGHS OF HOLLY

Deck the halls with boughs of holly,
Fa-la-la-la-la, la-la-la-la;
'Tis the season to be jolly,
Fa-la-la-la-la, la-la-la-la.
Don we now our gay apparel,
Fa-la-la-la-la, la-la-la-la.
Troll the ancient Christmas carol,
Fa-la-la-la-la, la-la-la-la!

See the blazing yule before us,
Fa-la-la-la-la, la-la-la-la;
Strike the harp and join the chorus,
Fa-la-la-la-la, la-la-la-la.
Follow me in merry measure,
Fa-la-la, fa-la-la, la-la-la.
While I tell of Christmas treasure,
Fa-la-la-la-la, la-la-la-la!

Fast away the old year passes,
Fa-la-la-la-la, la-la-la-la;
Hail the new, ye lads and lasses,
Fa-la-la-la-la, la-la-la-la.
Sing we joyous songs together,
Fa-la-la,
fa-la-la, la-la-la.
Heedless of the wind and weather,
Fa-la-la-la-la, la-la-la-la! □

O COME, ALL YE FAITHFUL

O come, all ye faithful, joyful and
triumphant,
O come ye, O come ye to Bethlehem;
Come and behold Him, born the
King of Angels;
O come, let us adore Him,
O come, let us adore Him,
O come, let us adore Him, Christ,
the Lord!

Sing, choirs of angels, sing in
exultation,
O sing, all ye citizens of heaven
above!
Glory to God, all glory in the
highest;
O come, let us adore Him,
O come, let us adore Him,
O come, let us adore Him, Christ,
the Lord!

Yea, Lord, we greet Thee, born this
happy morning,
Jesus, to Thee be all glory giv'n;
Word of the Father, now in flesh
appearing;
O come, let us adore Him,
O come, let us adore Him,
O come, let us adore Him, Christ,
the Lord!

☐

JOY TO THE WORLD!

Joy to the world! the Lord is come;
Let earth receive her King,
Let ev'ry heart prepare Him room,
And heav'n and nature sing,
And heav'n and nature sing,
And heav'n, and heav'n and nature
sing.

Joy to the world! the Saviour reigns;
Let men their sings employ;
While fields and floods, rocks, hills
and plains
Repeat the sounding joy,
Repeat the sounding joy,
Repeat, repeat the sounding joy.

He rules the world with truth and
grace,
And makes the nations prove
The glories of His righteousness,
And wonders of His love,
And wonders of His love,
And wonders, and wonders of His
love.

☐

SILENT NIGHT

Silent night, holy night!
All is calm, all is bright
Round yon Virgin Mother and Child.
Holy Infant so tender and mild,
Sleep in heavenly peace,
Sleep in heavenly peace.

☐

HARK! THE HERALD ANGELS SING

Hark! the herald angels sing,
"Glory to the newborn King;
Peace on earth, and mercy mild,
God and sinners reconciled!"
Joyful, all ye nations rise,
Join the triumph of the skies;
With th'angelic hosts proclaim,
"Christ is born in Bethlehem!"
Hark! the herald angels sing,
"Glory to the newborn King."

Christ, by highest heaven adored;
Christ, the everlasting Lord;
Come, Desire of Nations, come,
Fix in us Thy humble home.
Veiled in flesh the Godhead see;
Hail th'Incarnate Deity,
Pleased as man with man to dwell;
Jesus, our Emmanuel.
Hark! the herald angels sing,
"Glory to the newborn King."

Hail, the heav'n-born Prince of Peace!
Hail, the Sun of Righteousness!
Light and life to all He brings,
Ris'n with healing in His wings;
Mild He lays His glory by,
Born that man no more may die,
Born to raise the sons of earth,
Born to give them second birth;
Hark! the herald angels sing,
"Glory to the newborn King."

O LITTLE TOWN OF BETHLEHEM

O little town of Bethlehem,
How still we see thee lie!
Above thy deep and dreamless sleep
The silent stars go by;
Yet in thy dark street shineth
The everlasting Light;
The hopes and fears of all the years
Are met in thee tonight.

For Christ is born of Mary,
And gathered all above,
While mortals sleep, the angels keep
Their watch of wond'ring love.
O morning stars, together
Proclaim the holy birth,
And praises sing to God the King,
And peace to men on earth!

How silently, how silently,
The wondrous gift is giv'n!
So God imparts to human hearts
The blessings of His heav'n.
No ear may hear His coming,
But in this world of sin,
Where meek souls will receive Him still,
The Dear Christ enters in.

O holy Child of Bethlehem,
Descend on us, we pray;
Cast out our sin and enter in;
Be born in us today!
We hear the Christmas angels
The great glad tidings tell;
O come to us, abide with us
Our Lord Emmanuel!

THE TWELVE DAYS OF CHRISTMAS

On the first day of Christmas my
true love sent to me
  A partridge in a pear tree.

On the second day of Christmas my
true love sent to me
  Two turtle doves and a partridge
  in a pear tree.

On the third day of Christmas my
true love sent to me
  Three French hens, two turtle
  doves,
  And a partridge in a pear tree.

On the fourth day of Christmas my
true love sent to me
  Four calling birds, three French
  hens,
  Two turtle doves, and a partridge
  in a pear tree.

On the fifth day of Christmas my
true love sent to me
  Five gold rings!
  Four calling birds, three French
  hens,
  Two turtle doves, and a partridge
  in a pear tree.

On the sixth day of Christmas my
true love sent to me
  Six geese a-laying, Five gold rings!
  Four calling birds, three French
  hens,
  Two turtle doves, and a partridge
  in a pear tree.

On the seventh day of Christmas
my true love sent to me
  Seven swans a swimming
  etc.

On the eighth day of Christmas, my
true love gave to me
  Eight milking maids
  etc.

On the ninth day of Christmas my
true love sent to me
  Nine ladies dancing
  etc.

On the tenth day of Christmas my
true love sent to me
  Ten lords a-leaping
  etc.

On the eleventh day of Christmas
my true love gave to me
  Eleven pipers piping
  etc.

On the twelfth day of Christmas
my true love sent to me
  Twelve drummers drumming
  etc.   □

THE STAPLETONS

There are few families in Aspen that have lived here as long as the Stapletons. In 1981, they will celebrate their centennial—100 years in the Aspen area.

Sigrid and David Stapleton have raised a large family of five children— Kim, David, Dean, Stefanie and Dasha.

David's great grandparents, Tim and Ellen Stapleton, came to Aspen in 1881 in a covered wagon from Leadville, through Tin Cup, and over Taylor Pass. Tim and Ellen homesteaded on a ranch that is now the site of the Aspen airport.

Sigrid and her parents, Fred and Renate Braun, moved to Aspen in 1952 from Chicago. The Brauns are originally from Germany. Renate worked as a librarian for ten years in the Wheeler Opera House where the Chamber of Commerce is now located.

Fred is an engineer and has devoted many years of hard work to Mountain Rescue. He has spent many volunteer hours making the hut system a success for both locals and tourists to enjoy. The hut system is a series of mountain cabins that are scattered throughout the high country surrounding Aspen, which are available to people for overnight winter camping at a nominal fee.

The Stapletons celebrate Christmas on Christmas Eve, and Sigrid's German influence is dominant.

When the children were small, David and Sigrid decorated the tree on Christmas Eve, and before dinner let them see it all lit up for the first time. Dinner that night is traditionally a light fish meal, followed by a religious reading and singing of carols. Presents are opened one by one in front of the family. This special evening ends by attending Midnight Mass.

Christmas morning is spent at the home of David's parents, Bill and Louiva, where they have a traditional breakfast consisting of oyster stew, *potica* (a Yugoslavian bread), eggs, cookies and Tom-and-Jerrys.

The entire family is very close and they all get together to share a traditional turkey dinner on Christmas night.

The Stapletons celebrate Advent by hanging the Advent wreath over the dining room table and lighting one candle each Sunday preceding Christmas. The children each have their own Advent calendar, and open a window each day of the Advent weeks. Sigrid begins preparing baked goods a month before Christmas. Her specialties are fruitcakes, cookies, sweet breads and *stollen*. She also makes something different each year to give as gifts. Over the years, she has made friendship tea in colorful jars, homemade preserves, sachets, sweet breads, and tins filled with cookies and candies.

Sigrid's favorite part of Christmas is the preparation and making of things for other people.

For ornaments, they wrap bonbons in red paper and tie them to the tree with ribbons. The children are constantly snipping away the ornaments! Each child receives a new ornament every year for his or her own collection to take when they eventually leave home.   □

Celebration of Christmas

Celebration was not practical during the first years after Christ, for He was expected to return at any moment. Persecutions were taking place in Rome and the Christians were hiding.

In Turkey, Asia Minor, and Egypt, Epiphany was observed. Epiphany comes from the Greek work *Epiphaneia*, and commemorates the manifestation of God to the world in Jesus Christ, as revealed in His birth. Originally, Christ's birthdate was commonly honored on the same date as the Epiphany festival.

Some authorities believe that the Church assigned December 25 as the time for celebration as early as 320 A.D. The first known usage of the name "Christmas" dates back to 1038 and was coined by the English.

The celebration of Christmas has undergone extreme changes. During certain times, it was celebrated with

extravagance and gaiety, and other times, Christmas observance was attacked as a heathen practice. Our modern Christmas draws on these many past generations of change for certain elements of its observance.   □

THE BRENDLINGERS

Jack and Marsha have a close family built around their children—Kurt, Eric, Dina, and Kira. The way that they celebrate Christmas reflects this relationship.

The entire family gets together with a group of friends and spends a day cutting down their Christmas tree. This means a lot more to them than buying one.

The tree is decorated with smiling gingerbread men that Marsha bakes and the children decorate. Only one ginberbread man has a frown, and this single cookie is hidden on the tree by Jack. If this cookie is found by the children prior to Christmas Eve, Jack will continue to hide it. The child who finds the frown cookie on Christmas Eve gets to open the first gift that evening, and the first gift on Christmas Day. The excitement begins to grow.

Another Brendlinger tradition the children look forward to is one that Jack adapted from Denmark. On Christmas Eve, the family sits down to a turkey dinner by candlelight. For dessert, Marsha serves a creamy raisin rice pudding. She serves this special dessert in individual bowls. One of the bowls, picked randomly, has an almond hidden on the bottom. The child who finds the lone almond gets to choose what time the family rises on Christmas morning.

Christmas starts for the Brendlingers right after Thanksgiving. Jack and Marsha pick out a gift idea for friends and relatives. Over the next month, the entire family gets into the spirit of giving and everyone helps with this project. The day of Christmas Eve is spent delivering these gifts.

The Brendlingers have a family party the week before Christmas. Homemade invitations are sent out and the families invited start to prepare early. Each family must perform a program whether it be a skit, singing and dancing, or perhaps a poetry or story reading. The families really get involved. They plan, practice and often make their own costumes.

The meal consists of three kinds of soup, a variety of breads, salad and finger-food desserts. After dinner, the show begins. Marsha tells us, "Everyone enjoys it so much. The families work hard at pleasing and entertaining the others. Afterwards, the lights are turned off, candles are lit and everyone sings Christmas carols together. It then becomes rather serious. You really leave with a special feeling."

Another event the family looks forward to is their sledding party. Marsha serves a hot chile supper, and afterwards, everyone takes turns sledding from their home (up the West Buttermilk Road) down to the Buttermilk parking lot. The evening ends by their fireplace, drinking hot cider or hot spiced wine and reliving the fun of the evening.

On Christmas Eve, each child writes a letter to Santa Claus. The two younger girls put out a treat for him, usually cookies and milk.

Santa's gifts are the first ones opened in the morning. Before opening the gifts under the tree, the family has a breakfast of Eggs Benedict, fruit salad, homemade sweet rolls and hot chocolate.

The long-awaited gifts are opened one by one for all to see and appreciate. They spend many hours in this fashion. In the afternoon, the family takes a walk together.

Evening is spent playing games and eating a light supper of clam chowder and turkey sandwiches.

Marsha's family always packed a basket of food and then delivered it to a needy family on Christmas Eve. She has carried on this tradition with her church in Aspen.

Kris Kringle & Christmas Presents

The Kris Kringle legends, that the Christ child himself delivered presents, helped to establish Christmas Day as the occasion to exchange presents. At first, presents were very modest: a little money, cakes, apples, nuts, and small toys. Also included were useful things like clothes and self-improving items like Bibles, writing materials and books. These were the traditional Christmas presents of a child in the Middle Ages, arranged in their stockings with an apple at the top and an orange at the toe, and a new sixpence somewhere in between.

THE MACES

Stuart and Isabel Mace have lived in Aspen since 1947 and have built, owned and operated Toklat up at Ashcroft since 1948. Toklat is an Eskimo term that means "high valley cut by glaciers." This truly describes the location of their mountain home. Toklat was the answer to the Maces' dream of keeping arctic dog sledding adventures alive.

Stuart's interest in these arctic dogs began during World War II when he worked with the Tenth Mountain Division and Arctic Search and Rescue. Their mission was to retrieve planes and pilots that went down in the eastern and western routes of the arctic. They succeeded in using the aid of the arctic dog teams in their work. Stuart was so impressed with these dogs that he and Isabel brought them to Toklat where they have become a source of enjoyment for others.

The Maces became involved with work in Hollywood and at Ashcroft, filming their dog team. Along with Stuart, the dogs starred in the first color TV serial, *Sergeant Preston of the Yukon.* This production consumed more than three years of their lives.

Toklat began as a small guest lodge during the winter and summer seasons, lodging up to sixteen guests at a time. The unique and special meals they served to their guests led to a mail-order business. They sold their famous teas, homemade jams and jellies, sourdough starters, grains, and their savory wild mushroom soup. This mail-order business helped them survive during the slow off-seasons.

The Maces have five children—Greg, Lynne, Alan, Kent and Bruce. Their Christmas celebration is centered around their family life and a deep respect for the environment and conditions that surround them. Stuart recalls with fond memories the many times he took his family out into the woods with their dog team to properly cut a tree that needed to be thinned, never topping a tree or taking the most beautiful one in the forest for selfish reasons. The children learned quickly the meaning of saving our forests for the many generations to come. This tree-cutting event became a pleasurable family tradition over the years.

They always decorated their tree with as many handmade ornaments as possible, including popcorn, pinecones, plaster of Paris birds and animals, and cookies. Isabel always decorates Toklat by hanging boughs, pinecones with ribbons, and Stuart's homemade wreaths. Christmas is a relaxing and happy celebration for the Maces.

Nowadays, you'll find the Maces still as busy as ever. They are no longer in the lodge business, and their dogs have found a new home at Snowmass.

They do, however, serve a relaxed afternoon meal of homemade soup and bread during the winter months. Stuart operates a gallery at Toklat featuring his photography, and his many creations made of rare natural wood that include pictures, tables and Lazy Susans.

Stuart has devoted many hours of his time to teaching classes at the Aspen Center for Environmental Studies, which is located at Hallam Lake. Originally, Mrs. Paepcke established and donated the land for what is now a wildlife sanctuary. She had a dream of keeping alive wild animals and also teaching the public environmental awareness. She appointed Stuart to carry out these ideas.

Stuart is also on the Board of Advisors for Windstar, a non-profit organization founded by John Denver. The Windstar Project is seeking to create a harmonious living situation between man and nature.

⊓

The Christmas Tree

In 1605, in the City of Strasbourg, the fir tree was first presented as the holy tree of Christmas. It was decorated with wafers, gold foil, many-colored paper, apples and roses. It symbolized the tree in the Garden of Eden. Lighted and decorated trees date back many centuries. The Egyptians were known to bring the green date palms indoors because they represented life triumphant over death. The Romans trimmed trees with toys and trinkets during the Saturnalia.

After accepting Christianity, these people continued their winter rites but changed them to honor Christ. The evergreen tree has come to signify Christ bringing new life to the world after winter's long, dark days.

The Christmas tree tradition became popular in Germany in the 16th century, and gradually spread all over Europe and into the United States. □

THE HAYESES

Mary Eshbaugh moved to Aspen in 1952, at which time she met her husband-to-be, Jim, at the *Aspen Times*. Jim is a local silversmith, and is famous for his aspen leaf belt buckles.

Mary Eshbaugh Hayes is a reporter and photographer for *The Times*, and has written her weekly column, "Around Aspen," for many years, stating, "People in Aspen are where it's at." She felt that there was a need for a book about local Aspenites, both old and new. This idea inspired her to write the book *Aspen Potpourri*.

Christmas at the Hayeses is like a story out of a book. It starts for them at Thanksgiving, when they begin baking gingerbread men. Mary's brother, J.P. Eshbaugh, has kept a tradition of baking fruitcakes and sending them to the entire family every Thanksgiving. Boxes such as these, filled with homemade goodies, begin arriving at the Hayeses soon after Thanksgiving, and then, "We know it's Christmas!" From the German side of the family comes homemade clothes, toys and taffy. Then, from the English side, bayberry candles, cookies and books are traditional gifts. Everyone spends weeks before Christmas preparing gifts to send to one another. Pauli, the oldest daughter, continues the Hayes family tradition by stuffing handpainted cans

with homemade taffy, fudge and cookies to be sent to distant relatives.

A yearly event at the Hayeses is the hanging of their homemade Advent wreath.

They celebrate Christmas according to Mary's English and German influence, and from her two favorite childhood Christmas books by Tasha Tudor.

Throughout the Christmas season, Mary plays carols on the piano while the children fall asleep. To this day, her five children—Pauli, Elli, Lauri Le June, Clayton and Merri Jess (Bates) —appreciate and have warm memories of these times. The tree is decorated by all the children with ornaments they have made throughout the year. When the children were little, they spent weeks getting gifts ready for each other. They took great care with their projects, wanting Christmas to be special for the others.

Christmas morning finds the Hayeses opening stockings full of gifts, having a light breakfast of coffee and *stollen* and exchanging the many treasures from underneath the tree. □

Stir Up Sunday

Stir Up Sunday is the name for the Sunday before Advent. Traditionally, it was the last occasion on which Christmas puddings and cakes could be started if they were to be ready by December 25th. It was named Stir Up Sunday after the subject of the sermon in the church service for that day: "Stir up we beseech thee, O Lord, the wills of thy faithful people, that they plenteously bring forth the fruit of good works; may of thee be plenteously rewarded."

Plum porridge was the first type of plum pudding, and along with mince pies, it was not originally sweet at all, but made with meat. It is still traditional to bury a silver coin or charm in the pudding. All the family should take turns stirring the pudding and make a wish at the same time. Then the coin should be added, plus a ring and a thimble; the coin is to bring fortune, the ring a marriage, and the thimble a blessed life.

□

THE SKAERINGSSON FAMILY

Úlfar and Hjördis came to Aspen the winter of 1960 from Reykjavik, Iceland. Úlfar began as a ski instructor for Stein Eriksen at Aspen Highlands. He is now the head instructor for the Aspen Ski School on Aspen Mountain. Hjördis has taught skiing at Buttermilk Mountain for ten years and is known there as "Queen Bee." They have three children—Áslaug, Markus and Edda, all of whom are very involved with sports.

In Iceland, the winters are very dark, allowing only five hours of daylight. Christmas is a very happy holiday, for it emits light both visually and spiritually to the people.

Hjördis tells us that they put up their tree on the night of December 23rd. This night in Iceland is called Thorlaksmessa, named after a saint.

They start celebrating Christmas Eve by first attending Mass, and then having a large traditional Icelandic dinner consisting of smoked leg of lamb with small white potatoes served with a white sauce and nutmeg; sweet and sour cabbage; sweet peas and carrots; and, for dessert, rice pudding. Hjördis always has food sent over from

Iceland so they can continue to have an authentic traditional meal.

The family then opens their gifts. Hjördis sighs, "We stay up well past midnight eating delicious pastries and tortes and drinking coffee. Our tree is lovely, decorated with cookies and handmade ornaments, and, of course, all lit up with real candles." They make cornucopias, which are paper cones, fill them with treats and hang them on the tree. Hjördis explains, "In Iceland, we celebrate the twelve days before Christmas. The children put a shoe in the window for these twelve nights in hopes that Jolasveinar, or gnomes, will leave them a gift."

The Skaeringssons get up late on Christmas Day and sit down to a fancy, mid-day meal of ptarmigan, a savory wild bird. Friends and family spend the day together. Candles are lit throughout the day. The light they cast brings a special feeling to all.

Another Icelandic tradition they celebrate is the Second Day of Christmas. This is December 26th, and is a day devoted to simply being carefree. Hjördis tells us, "Christmas is a very religious day. The next day we go to a party or a dance." □

Lights on Christmas Trees

Light has been a long-time symbol of Christian joy which dispels the darkness of paganism. Lights have always accompanied joyous occasions and festivities, for light represents faith. Candles symbolize Christ as the Light of the World. Martin Luther is known to have placed tapers, small wax candles, on the tree.

The story is told of how he was working on Christmas Eve under a clear night sky lit by thousands of stars. The sight moved him so that when he returned home, he took an uprooted fir tree with him and fixed candles to its branches to remind children of the heavens from which Christ descended to save us.

Electric lights in many cases, but not all, have come to replace candles on trees.

However, candles are still a major part of the Christmas celebration. They are still seen on mantels, tables, in churches, and being carried by carolers in the night. □

Lou and Lynne have been in Aspen twenty-eight years. They met when Lou was giving art classes and Lynne was his student. Their four children—Raoul, Shauna, Andre and Pierre—were all born here.

The whole family is extremely artistic and make many of their Christmas presents including handmade cards, ornaments and their special fruitcake.

Lou, who is environmentally conscious, takes special care in picking out their Christmas tree. When he comes upon a cluster of evergreens, he chooses a tree that is being crowded. This tree is usually sparsely branched on one side which is the side that they face into the corner of their home. They then decorate it with bird ornaments collected from various parts of the world.

The special closeness of the Wille family is symbolized in the making of little gifts and poems for each other. They have a small "pocket tree" on which each of them has a pocket, and they exchange paper gifts such as poems and magazine subscriptions.

Lynne keeps cards from previous years that are special. She makes a tree on the wall with these cards and decorates it with pine boughs. She has constructed a wreath out of various beautiful bird feathers which she hangs on their front door.

Pierre takes pride in his decorated Christmas boxes and wrappings. When he really gets into a creative mood, he makes his packages resemble various animals! He has built his own version of Rudolph who guards their mountain retreat over the holiday season. □

Decorations

The tradition of decorating the house with holly and ivy, and other evergreens, is a practice which can be traced back to the Romans. Evergreens were a token of good luck to the Romans who brought them into their homes during the winter celebrations.

Holly, with its needle-sharp leaves and blood-red berries, became associated with Christ's crown of thorns, and represented the blood. There's a story that tells of the first Christmas night, when the shepherds went to the manger. A small lamb who followed them was caught by the holly thorns, and the red berries are the blood drops that froze on the branches that night. There are more than 150 varieties of holly. Conveniently, it grows in practically all the countries of the world. Because it bears fruit in the winter, holly has come to symbolize immortality.

Mistletoe comes from ancient Britain where it was the sacred plant of the Druids. The Arch Druid supposedly cut the mistletoe with a sickle each year in November. Elaborate ceremonies took place, and the mistletoe was divided among the people, who took it home to hang over their doors. They believed it to work miracles of healing, to protect against witchcraft, and to bring fertility to the land and the people. Kissing under the mistletoe has become a custom. Lads may claim a kiss from the girl who happens to be under it. The lad removes a berry and gives it to the girl. No more kisses are available when all the berries are taken.   □

THE DE PAGTERS

Jack and Anneke De Pagter arrived in Aspen from Holland in 1949. A year later (1950), Jack built the Holland House, which is located at the base of Aspen Mountain. Together, with their daughter, Yasmine, they have worked hard at making their lodge a warm and friendly place to stay. They have established a clientele of guests from all over the world who return each year to spend the Christmas season together.

Since moving to the United States, the De Pagters have Americanized their Dutch customs.

Each year, the guests begin arriving a week or two before Christmas. The Christmas tree, which is the main focal point of the lodge at this special time, is decorated by the family and all their guests. Being away from home at this time doesn't seem to matter, as the Christmas spirit is in the air, and there is a true feeling of family.

Christmas Eve for the De Pagters is traditionally set aside to spend with their employees. A dinner of oyster stew is enjoyed by everyone.

Anneke decorates the table for Christmas breakfast with greenery and candles to assure a special feeling. The guests feast on homemade *stollen*, a traditional Christmas bread, bacon, eggs, and coffee, before heading for the slopes for a day of skiing. Some of the less enthusiastic skiers stay and help

Anneke and Yasmine prepare for the evening party.

Returning from the slopes, the guests enjoy taking special care to dress up for the Christmas party. The party starts at 5 and everyone partakes of hot wine and hors d'oeuvres. The guests are from Argentina, Australia, New Zealand, Holland, Germany, Sweden, Chile and England. They love standing around the piano singing traditional Christmas carols in their own tongue.

Then the grab bag, which has always been a source for great fun and entertainment, begins. The guests, having drawn a name the week before, take great pains in choosing just the right gift. The gift is kept at under $5 and aims at each person's soft spot, in jest. Dr. Phil Freedman, who has been coming to the Holland House for eighteen years, and met and married his wife Anne in Aspen, acts as the MC. He keeps the atmosphere of merriment and camaraderie high.

They stay up singing, telling stories and laughing until they can no longer keep their eyes open, knowing that the next day is a ski day. □

St. Nicholas

All over the world, children know St. Nicholas. In America, he is known as Santa Claus. In Europe, millions of children celebrate the beginning of Christmas on December 6th, his special saint's day.

His story began hundreds of years ago in the eastern part of the world known as the Cradle of Christianity. Nicholas was the Bishop of Myra, a city in the province of Lycia, in Asia Minor. Though his birthdate is unknown, he grew up in the town of Patara where he became noted for his Christian piety. When the elderly Bishop of Myra died, Nicholas was chosen, though still very young, to take his place.

We are told that he was generous, kind and full of courage. He was able to win many souls to Christianity by his good example. There are various stories from the past that tell of miracles he performed and also tell of his incredible kindness to the poor of his diocese. There are many reasons why he was gradually adopted as Father Christmas. A legend that is most responsible for his reputation as a giver of gifts is one about three unmarried daughters. A poor nobleman had three daughters who were unmarried because he was unable to give them each a dowry. In that day, it was the custom for the father of the bride to present a dowry to her future husband. When Father Nicholas heard of their plight, he was overcome with sympathy, and one night, while passing by their home, he dropped a bag of gold through an open window. Not once, but thrice, St. Nicholas made this generous gesture. All three daughters were properly wed. It is said that when the third bag of gold was dropped in the window, Nicholas was spotted by the father. Although he showered the Bishop with thanks, Nicholas pleaded that he keep it a secret. And so it was that when the story came out in later years, Nicholas became known as the secret giver of gifts.

St. Nicholas Day in many parts of the world is celebrated on December 6th, the date of his death. Since December 6th is close to Christmas Day, he became associated with that holiday.

On the Eve of St. Nicholas Day, the children left gifts of hay and carrots on their doorstep for his white horse. It seemed only natural that he would surprise them with gifts in return. And so it became customary to exchange gifts on this day. After several hundred years, in many countries, this custom of giving was moved to Christmastime. For most of the children of the world, St. Nicholas began to make his visits to earth on Christmas Eve.

When the Dutch settled in the New World, they brought St. Nicholas along. And when they spoke lovingly of good old "San Nicolaas," it must have been very much like "Sanna Claus" to the other children. It was not long before the American name of Santa Claus was adopted by the children for this kind and generous old fellow. Though his appearance has changed, there is still that loving spirit present in his character of that beloved saint who lived hundreds of years ago.

PART II

□

Songs, Poetry & Stories

Music and stories relive the meaning of Christmas. For within these arts lies the magic of feelings and keeping alive the spirit of this wondrous holiday. Without them, the gaiety, the remembering of times past, and the feelings of the present and future would simply not exist.

We found that Christmas has been a subject written about since its beginning and it's nice to know that it has not been forgotten in our age.

We are grateful for the opportunity to present to you songs, poetry, and stories by Aspenites.

This section of our book begins with two songs taken from the Muppets' Christmas album: "Alfie, The Christmas Tree," by John Denver, and "The Christmas Wish," by Danny Wheetman. The substance of their contemporary messages speaks for themselves. Both John and Danny are from the Aspen area. Busy as they are, they always manage to find the time to perform in concerts that benefit the many organizations of our town.

Following these songs appear three poems and a short romantic story by three Aspen women. Then we give you the chance to read some works by Aspen school children.

We end this section with two of our most favorite traditional works: *A Visit from St. Nicholas,* and Virginia's famous letter to the editor of the *New York Sun* doubting the authenticity of Santa Claus.　　　　　　　　□

ALFIE, THE CHRISTMAS TREE

by John Denver

Did you ever hear the story of
  the Christmas tree
Who just didn't want to change
  the show?
He liked living in the woods
  and playing with squirrels;
He liked icicles and snow;
He liked wolves and eagles
  and grizzly bears
And critters and creatures
  that crawled.
Why, bugs were some of his
  very best friends,
Spiders and ants and all.

Now, that's not to say that he
  never looked down
On the vision of twinkling lights;
Or on mirrored bubbles and
  peppermint canes
And a thousand other delights.
And he often had dreams of
  tiny reindeer
And a jolly old man in a sleigh
Full of toys and presents and
  wonderful things,
And the story of Christmas Day.

Oh, Alfie believed in Christmas
  all right.
He was full of Christmas cheer
All of each and every day

And all throughout the year.
To him it was more than a
  special time,
Much more than a special day.
It was more than a beautiful story;
It was a special kind of way.

You see, some folks have never
  heard a jingle bell ring
And they've never heard of
  Santa Claus.
They've never heard the story
  of the Son of God;
And that made Alfie pause.
Did that mean that they'd never
  know of peace on earth?
Or the brotherhood of man?
Or know how to love, or know
  how to give?
If they can't no one can.

You see, life is a very special
  kind of thing,
Not just for a chosen few;
But for each and every living,
  breathing thing,
Not just me and you.
So in your Christmas prayers this year,
Alfie asked me if I'd ask you
To say a prayer for the wind,
  and the water and the wood,
And those who live there too!

THE CHRISTMAS WISH

by Danny Allen Wheetman

For I have held the precious
gift that love brings,
Even though I never saw a
Christmas star.
I know there is a light, I have
felt it burn inside,
And I have seen it shining
from afar.

Christmas is the time to come
together,
A time to put all diff'rences
aside.
And I reach out my hand to the
family of man, To share the joy I feel
at Christmas time.

For the truth that binds us all
together,
I would like to say a simple
prayer;
That at this special time, you
will have true peace of mind,
And love to last throughout
the coming year.

I don't know if you believe in
Christmas,
Or if you have presents underneath
the Christmas tree,
But if you believe in love, that
will be more than enough,
For you to come and celebrate
with me.

And if you believe in love,
That will be more than enough,
For peace to last throughout the
coming year,
And peace on earth will last
throughout the year.

It happens to most of us once in our lives, that Christmas comes around and we haven't a dime. It happened to us shortly after we were married. This was my sole gift to my husband.

IF I COULD GIVE

by Diana Ryan

Before you peek inside this box
  There's something I should say
I could not fit it all you see
  I hope you don't dismay.

There is a trick I must reveal
  to opening this gift
To catch a glimpse of what it holds
  I say, you must be swift!

Although the seams are bursting
  and the ribbons are so taut
The contents could escape so fast
  And you would know it naught.

Well, now I know you cannot wait
  to open this at last
And so, remember well my love
  you must, you must be fast!

Ah, you were not quick enough!
  However it's not gone—
I just can't keep it held inside
  especially not for long.

No matter what I put it in
  it wants to overflow
The universe is far too large
  to package up, you know.

But still, I took them one by one
  the sky, the moon, the star
And when I had them all at hand
  I put them in a jar.

Now, since that was so long ago
  I put the jar away
To wait until the time had come
  and now, on Christmas Day—

I found the jar about to burst
  and much to my surprise
Upon a closer look inside
  The sky had turned to skies

The midnight blue I'd packed away
  had brought on scarlet dawn
And next in line was golden dusk
  to warn the day was gone.

And then, of course, to follow
  dusk
  was silent, noble moon
Whose fuller shape had proved
  to me
I'd picked him far too soon.

37

The stars had spent the
    timeless days
by multiplying fast
And point to point they
    held their breath
    'til Christmas Eve was past.

So late last night, while
    you did sleep   .
The universe came out.
And though they danced around
    a lot
I bid them not to shout.

I said they were my gift to you.
    They did not understand.
"To represent my love," I said
    but that, they felt too grand.

The vastness of my love,
    they said,
    they knew it to be such
That stretch and stretch as
    they might try
They could not spread that much.

I told them that it mattered not
    that they were all I had
I tried to cheer them up,
    you know
    They felt so very bad—

I bid them—climb into the box
    adverse as they may be
They said they would, if first
    one thing
    I promised to agree—

That when the lid was lifted off
    that homeward they could fly
And spread themselves to
    places new
    the stars, the moon, the sky.

And so, in relevance, to you
    in ways that you can see
The universe is out today
    I promised to agree.

□

HOPE FOR THE SINGLE GIRL

We found a few delightful Christmas customs for the young lady who wishes to improve her love life. These customs are some of the many of a superstitious nature practiced years ago. Few times of the year serve the young woman better than Christmastide. The single girl may approach the door of the henhouse on Christmas Eve. Knock loudly, and wait. The chances for marriage during the coming year are poor if a hen cackles first.

If, however, a cock crows, her future will be filled with good things.

If a single girl puts lead in a cup of water at midnight on Christmas Eve, the shape it takes will determine the profession of her husband: nails for a carpenter, horseshoes for a blacksmith, etc.

To see her future husband, a single girl can make a dough-cake in silence, place it on the hearth, and prick her initials on the surface. If she watches, at midnight on Christmas Eve, she will see her future husband enter the room, go to the hearth, and prick his initials next to hers.

If she walks backwards toward a pear tree on Christmas morning, circles it three times, then looks up, she will see the image of her future husband among the branches. She can also see his image if she picks twelve sage leaves from the garden on Christmas Eve.

The loveliest idea is for the single girl to keep the rose she plucked on Midsummer's Day. On Christmas morning, it will still be as fresh as when she picked it and if she wears it to church, her future husband will come to take it from her.

□

KAREN BATISTA

Karen Batista wrote a poem about herself.

"I'm an old fashioned girl—
  a modern day
pearl—full of life and
  laughter...
living back before the
  hereafter...
  A Christmas kid and
lover of Santa Claus..."Up
  on the
housetops and reindeer paws..."
  Snowdrops and sleighbells
...a chorus of holiday things...
forever tugging on her sentimental
heart strings."

These few lines from her poem describe this romantic Aspen lady who lives in a log cabin she helped build in the woods outside of town.

Karen moved to Aspen on Halloween night in 1964 from California. She's had several jobs which vary from working at the *Aspen Times*, to being Sam Caudill's secretary, to being a receptionist at Bernee's & Larry's Hairstyling. Currently, she is a legal secretary. She enjoys skiing, mountain climbing, skating, cooking and sewing, and just being a lady.

Being a writer, she describes her Christmas Eve wedding.

This is one of those "...Once upon a time..." stories. I guess that's how I should begin this reminiscence of my Aspen wedding—I was a December bride—a July-born, hopelessly romantic girl from the Arrowhead woods of Southern California who, on a fine spring day in Aspen, stumbled into a tall, dark and handsome (blue-eyed!) fellow from the East Coast, and at the time, more particularly, a fisherman from Cape Cod, Massachusetts.

After a summer courtship of fun and love, Brad proposed marriage, and I happily accepted. He said the date of the wedding was my choice, and being one of the original Christmas kids, I picked Christmas Eve. It was then the beginning of November and the six weeks of nervous and crazy preparation began.

Aspen town was quaint in 1965 with only one department store, one fabric shop, one dentist, one of this and that, and lots of "none of many things!" I didn't know all of the things you had to do to get married, and luckily for me, my best friend and matron of honor, Sandy Pelletier, helped me put it all together! I sent away for six yards of lace netting for my veil and a pearl-studded crown, and began having Shirley and Suzi at The Emporium make my wedding dress. We went to see Sandy Sanderson, a local silversmith, about having slalom rings made (I never dreamed of diamonds somehow), so we had several "sterling" ring fittings in preparation for the final rings to be made out of "white gold." I wrote to at least seven florists everywhere trying to find gardenias and white poinsettias—I tried "both" beauty shops in town trying to get a soft, wispy French roll, and sent away to Spiegel's for sparkly Christmas shoes.

The town was getting snowier all the time and Christmas lights blossomed all over the place. I am now calling my folks in California nearly every other day—help this—help that—don't talk too long—don't cry—don't be nervous!

I had my hair done at Amelia's the morning of Christmas Eve. I was extremely nervous because my shoes hadn't arrived, none of the florists could guarantee fresh flowers, and rumor had it that Brad (who was a ski patrolman at Aspen Highlands) was going to be locked up inside the Loges Peak lift shack at the top of the mountain on Christmas Eve! Meanwhile, my folks were busy decorating Sandy and Romeo's home with red and green crepe paper streamers for the reception.

I managed to remember to pick up the wedding rings and Brad's pants from the cleaners. But an hour before the wedding, I realized I still didn't have any shoes! I sent Mom to Mathew's Drugs for shoe makeup and we cleverly disguised a pair of "Aspen's-only-department-store-vintage" navy blue pumps!

Bless the Aspen Community Church —it was still there. Bless my family— Dad brought me an orchid. Bless the ring bearers, Boone and Robin Caudill —complete with red hair, freckles and smiles, and the two Santa Claus elf dolls holding our rings, as we'd forgotten the pillows. And bless Sandy! We had given her my crown and the six yards of netting the night before, and she appeared with the most beautiful veil I'd ever seen—even prettier than the ones in *Bride Magazine!*

The altar in the church was beautiful and painted dark blue with white stars. I couldn't believe it because I love stars so much! Candles were lit and set among pine boughs, and they even had a decorated Christmas tree. The organ began to play and the stage was set. Dad and I held each other up going down the aisle. Brad walked in dressed in a red Scotch tartan plaid jacket, his freshly pressed pants, and a big smile. We stood before the minister and my left leg began to shake—I couldn't get it to stop! Our fingers got swollen so the rings didn't go on very well, and I am told that I was in such a spell that I interrupted the minister to look up at Brad and say, "I love you..." I could hear Dad crying as he stood up alongside of us—and eventually, we got to kiss and my leg stopped shaking!

It was dark when we left the church, and we were greeted by handfuls of rice. To our shock and surprise, friends outside had a sleigh waiting with two big white horses harnessed in bells, and our friend Louis McCutcheon was waiting with the reins! Brad hoisted me up, and friends and family piled in as well! Sandy had made a huge "Just Married" sign for the side of the sleigh and off we went down Bleeker Street singing "Jingle Bells." I wondered if Tinkerbell was up in the sky making it all happen. I never knew how beautiful a sleigh with bells and horses' hooves could sound!

We arrived at Sandy and Romeo's in old-fashioned style. Sandy's tree was covered with candy canes, tinsel and homemade pink and green cookie ornaments, and the Christmas paper cups seemed to hold the champagne even prettier than the fancy glasses we could not afford.

The evening was ended with an elegant dinner at Stromberg's Restaurant (now Chisholm's Saloon!) with lots of toasts and laughter.

We left for our honeymoon on Christmas Day. We had heard there was a ski area in Redstone, forty miles away. It was a lovely drive with Christmas lights blinking from snug mountain homes, and the quaint old Redstone Lodge was lit up for the season. It was a wonderful place to spend a honeymoon, watching the softly falling snow, and learning about each other.

It was a Christmas that I will always look back on with fond memories. □

PINE TINSEL

by Karen Batista

Tinsel of pine
  clear and slender prisms
hang from snowy branches
  in rhyme.

Glistening in the daytime sun
  and scattered about our
mountain ski runs.

Cool and quiet to the sight,
  a pencil sized shimmer
when moonlight warms the night.

A beauteous wink of nature
  clinging like silver—yet— free
decorate the branches of pine
  on our wilderness Christmas trees.

ONCE A YEAR

by Linda Liddell

Ain't no telling about Christmas
no more, what with it being all
packaged and boxed
papered and ribboned
makes me wonder
who's hiding, what,
and which 'whats'
from whom
and what really is
hiding underneath
those short circuit lights
ornaments and popcorn
hangin from the tree
what else is the present
for Uncle Bob—

green fuzzy slippers
and that red-haired doll
for Betty Anne—
none of it will be remembered
come next spring.

Gift wrapped love
and no one is sure
exactly how to untie it,
it's a sneaky way,
to say "I love you"
and Christmas don't come
but once a year.

We thought it would be fun to create a poetry and short story contest for the children who live in Aspen. Children have such wonderful imaginations, and a contest is always a good incentive. Here are our favorites.

AN EVERLASTING GIFT OF LOVE

by Sarah Aley—Grade 8

One night as I was walking down to our barn, the full moon shone luminously over the bright sparkling snow. I could see the dainty hoof prints in the powdery snow of struggling deer in the winter's bitterness. As I neared the barn, every shadow and moving object was visible in the brightness. A blustery wind blew fierce and cold across my already numb cheeks. Upon entering the barn, I was hit with the realization of the extreme warmth compared to outside. It was Christmas Eve. All the animals stirred restlessly in their stalls. Comet, our jersey milk cow, was standing in the fresh clean straw, letting out barely audible "moos." Then there was Prince Mouse, pawing nervously at the bare dirt that was his night-time home. Snowflake, the white goat, was scampering back and forth in her pen, bleating. Wilbur and Wallace, our pigs, lay unaffected as usual in their clean straw. I could hear a few cackles once in a while from the chickens. As I groped my way over to the feed bins I became aware of an increasing peacefulness. Comet mooed, Prince Mouse neighed, Snowflake baahed, and Wilbur and Wallace jumped to their hooves right away, a once-in-a-lifetime feat. I ran quickly outside, for some reason, feeling that something was waiting out there for me. I surveyed the pasture, abundant with the light of a billion stars. Everything was so beautiful, it seemed as if the slightest noise could break it. Just at that moment, I heard a far-off noise that sounded over and over again. I walked nonchalantly into the barn, mounted Prince Mouse, and we were off. Off into a world that seemed to be made of glass. As we approached the sound at a faster speed, I caught a glance of a sleigh, lighted by a lantern. Nearing it, I could make out the faint image of a man, with birds and beasts all around him. When he saw me, he quickly fumbled with a gunny sack. As I disembarked my pony, he walked over to me in a gentle way, calming all my fears. He handed me a small lamb whose woolly fur stood on end.

He was an elderly gentleman, maybe about sixty-five years old. His silvery hair curled handsomely around his face. Under his darkly tanned and weatherbeaten face, I could feel a genuine love. He spoke, "Please take this little lamb, for I am not capable of taking care of it myself." As I took it, I could feel her snuggle her small head in the crook of my arm. I was not looking at the lamb, but at the old man as he rode away on his sleigh. As he did, the rabbits ran back to their holes, the birds to their nests, the coyotes and foxes to their lairs. All holding a new and eternal respect for each other.

We still have that memory of that lamb in our hearts, although we had her only a short time.

That night as I walked home, I felt that I knew the true meaning of Christmas. The steeple bell tolled as the trees blinked on and off their warming colors. □

OH, CHRISTMAS TREE
by Allyson Mendenhall—Grade 6

Eight days before Christmas, my family and I set off for Lenado to cut our traditional twenty-foot Christmas tree. Most families wouldn't consider this a big event, but my family does, which I think is nice. We started out about 7:30 a.m. with the Suburban packed to the brim, with Mom, Dad, kids, dogs, and Grandma. We had packed a huge lunch the night before, because last year we didn't have enough food and became very hungry. The dogs behaved very well on the long drive. We were very happy with them until we discovered they had eaten our lunch, which was in the back of the car.

We finally reached the area in which we were allowed to cut our tree. The Forest Service officer stopped us to collect our money. My Dad only had a dollar, but it cost one dollar twenty-five. The officer could not let us by without paying the full price, so we discussed it and made a deal. We told him he could come in any time to our shop, Wax & Wicks, for a glass of hot spiced cider.

We parked the car in the small parking lot, and started walking down the narrow path. I was exhausted after the first thirty feet. Gretchen and Luther, our dogs, had a bit of trouble running in the snow too. My brother shouted to Dad, "Hey Dad, look at that tree way up there," pointing with his finger! We all agreed that it was a nice tree so my Dad climbed up to take a look at it. We didn't realize we were making him climb three hundred feet in deep snow. He yelled down to us, "It's much too tall, but there is a nice one right next to it!" We couldn't see it, but trusted his choice so we yelled to him that he should go ahead and cut it down. We heard him saw the tree down, and then he appeared out of nowhere dragging a beautiful tree, just the perfect size and shape.

We had a beautiful and perfect tree, but were having a hard time dragging it back to the car. We tried harnessing it to the dogs, but they couldn't drag it either. So all five of us were stuck dragging it. We stopped every five minutes to rest our cramped backs. Finally, we got to the car. Now we had to lift it onto the car. Boy, was it hard, but we did it. We strapped the tree on with ropes and twine and then piled in the car.

We left Lenado dirty, tired, hungry, wet and sweaty. We were a sight. The dogs were leaning over the seat licking and breathing in our faces. All of a sudden we heard a crack, and the whole tree slid down the front windshield, causing us to slide into a ditch. We all jumped out of the car. My Dad strapped on the tree again while all of us pushed the car back onto the road. Once again we piled in the car and continued our journey home. Once we were home, we unloaded the car and went inside. We had a very late lunch, took hot baths, and went to sleep. I hope this tradition carries on for all the years to come. □

THE NIGHT BEFORE IN ASPEN, COLORADO

by Martha Dayton, Grade 8

"Hey David, what time is it?" After I heard no reply, I turned to find him looking in the window of Gazebo Gifts. "David, what time is it?" I repeated. "Four o'clock, why?"

"Just wondering," I answered.

The two of us were wandering around Aspen finishing up our last-minute shopping. It was the night before Christmas. The snow that was falling lightly seemed to have a covenant with the smoke billowing from the chimneys of condos and houses. It was a beautiful sight. All the windows were bright with Christmas decor. As we passed La Tortue, I glanced up toward the North of Nell Condominiums to see many trees covered with aged, but gorgeous, ornaments.

As we ambled past the bus station, I had this feeling of sympathy for the drivers of those monstrous buses. We decided to stop in P'Nuts, a great kid's store, to buy my little girl an Obermeyer turtleneck. We passed the Arrow Shop (which was closed) and some man was knocking on the door asking, "Please let me in. I just need one little thing."

We continued on and passed a little girl licking a candy cane. We headed toward the mall. What a sight! All the lights had red and green paper wrapped around them and all the windows had lights or similar decor. I was astounded. I stumbled and fell, which partially woke me up from my daze. We entered the doors of Wax and Wicks to be greeted with a delicious cup of hot cider. It warmed me up. David bought his wife a candle. Two more stops and we would be ready to go back to our warm and cheery condominiums. The first, across the mall, happened to be Timberline Books. I had to buy myself a 1980 calendar to remember Aspen.

Last, but not least, we had to make a stop at The Chocolate Soldier to get some little Santas and Christmas candies for the kids. I even bought myself a square of fudge. When we finished, we went home to the Fifth Avenue Condos. It was a glorious sight to enter the door and see the happiness in the room, but nothing is as special as the sight of the town of Aspen on Christmas Eve. □

SANTA'S DILEMMA
by Gretchen Cole, Grade 8

Christmas had come,
In the dark of December,
It was a cold month
As I remember.

The forest was filled
With deep crisp snow,
And the long ride home
Was a sharp, cold blow.

Toward my house I turned the gate
To find a horrifying disaster,
Santa's big red sleigh
Was stuck in my pasture.

For a solution
I wracked my brain,
I could not think,
I was going insane.

Santa yelped in fear
As I jumped to my feet.
I got down from my wagon
But the snow was waist deep.

The challenge was tough
As I trudged and stomped
As I came upon Santa,
It went kerplomp.

I quickly worked and
Untangled the mess,
Santa was grateful
To me he would bless.

I invited Santa, reindeer and all,
In for hot cider.
They drank, and laughed
Then all seemed brighter.

They thanked me greatly
And took off with great joys
To make their Christmas
    deliveries
Of candles and toys.

SNOWY WINTER DAY
by Sarah Sterling, Grade 7

---

*J*ust you and me ride in a
    sleigh,
On a snowy, white winter day.
We ride under the crescent moon,
and over the white hills,
Through the big oak trees,

to the glistening frozen pond.
We skate along the smooth, clear
    ice
and sing a merry tune,
But know this dream will be
    over soon!

SANTA SANTA
by Brian Davies, Grade 5

---

*S*anta Santa I believe
That you will be here
Christmas Eve.
To fill my stocking
By the fire,
With all the things
That I desire.

Santa, Santa, please bring me
Some fruit, candy
and I'd love a
baby cougar.

A VISIT FROM ST. NICHOLAS

by Clement Clarke Moore

Twas the night before Christmas, when all through the house
Not a creature was stirring, not even a mouse.
The stockings were hung by the chimney with care,
In hopes that St. Nicholas soon would be there.

The children were nestled all snug in their beds,
While visions of sugar-plums danced in their heads;
And mamma in her kerchief, and I in my cap,
Had just settled our brains for a long winter's nap—

When out on the lawn there arose such a clatter
I sprang from my bed to see what was the matter.
Away to the window I flew like a flash,
Tore open the shutter, and threw up the sash.

The moon on the breast of the new-fallen snow
Gave a lustre of midday to objects below;
When what to my wondering eye should appear
But a miniature sleigh and eight tiny reindeer,

With a little old driver, so lively and quick,
I knew in a moment it must be St. Nick!
More rapid than eagles his coursers they came,
And he whistled and shouted and called them by name.

"Now, Dasher! now, Dancer! now, Prancer and Vixen!
On, Comet! on, Cupid! on, Donder and Blitzen!—
To the top of the porch, to the top of the wall,
Now, dash away, dash away, dash away all."

As dry leaves that before the wild hurricane fly,
When they meet with an obstacle mount to the sky,

So, up to the housetop the coursers they flew,
With a sleigh full of toys—and St. Nicholas, too.

And then, in a twinkling, I heard on the roof
The prancing and pawing of each little hoof.
As I drew in my head and was turning around,
Down the chimney St. Nicholas came with a bound:

He was dressed all in fur from his head to his foot,
And his clothes were all tarnished with ashes and soot:
A bundle of toys he had flung on his back,
And he looked like a peddler just opening his pack.

His eyes, how they twinkled! his dimples, how merry!
His cheeks were like roses, his nose like a cherry;
His droll little mouth was drawn up like a bow,
And the beard on his chin was as white as the snow.

The stump of a pipe he held tight in his teeth,
And the smoke, it encircled his head like a wreath.
He had a broad face and a little round belly
That shook, when he laughed, like a bowl full of jelly.

He was chubby and plump—a right jolly old elf:
And I laughed when I saw him, in spite of myself;
A wink of his eye, and a twist of his head,
Soon gave me to know I had nothing to dread.

He spoke not a word, but went straight to his work,
And filled all the stockings: then turned with a jerk,
And laying his finger aside of his nose,
And giving a nod, up the chimney he rose.

He sprang to his sleigh, to his team gave a whistle,
And away they all flew like the down of a thistle.
But I heard him exclaim, ere they drove out of sight,
"Happy Christmas to all, and to all a good-night!"

YES, VIRGINIA, THERE IS A SANTA CLAUS

by Francis P. Church, The New York Sun, *September 21, 1897*

Dear Editor:
I am 8 years old.
Some of my little friends say there is no Santa Claus. Papa says "If you see it in The Sun *it's so."*
Please tell me the truth; is there a Santa Claus?
Virginia O'Hanlon

Virginia, your little friends are wrong. They have been affected by the skepticism of a skeptical age. They do not believe except they see. They think that nothing can be which is not comprehensible by their little minds. All minds, Virginia, whether they be men's or children's, are little. In this great universe of ours man is a mere insect, an ant, in his intellect, as compared with the boundless world about him, as measured by the intelligence capable of grasping the whole of truth and knowledge.

Yes, Virginia, there is a Santa Claus. He exists as certainly as love and generosity and devotion exist, and you know that they abound and give to your life its highest beauty and joy. Alas! how dreary would be the world if there were no Santa Claus! It would be as dreary as if there were no Virginias. There would be no childlike faith then, no poetry, no romance to make tolerable this existence. We should have no enjoyment, except in sense and sight. The eternal light with which childhood fills the world would be extinguished.

Not believe in Santa Claus! You might as well not believe in fairies! You might get your papa to hire men to watch in all the chimneys on Christmas Eve to catch Santa Claus, but even if they did not see Santa Claus coming down, what would that prove? Nobody sees Santa Claus, but that is no sign that there is no Santa Claus. The most real things in the world are those that neither children nor man can see.

No Santa Claus! Thank God, he lives, and he lives forever. A thousand years from now, Virginia, nay, ten times ten thousand years from now, he will continue to make glad the heart of children. ☐

50

PART III

Recipes

The Christmas season is the time of year for eating, drinking and good cheer. With help from our friends, we proudly bring you their favorite Christmas recipes from around the world. □

THE THUILLIERS

Maurice and Ann Thuillier have lived in Aspen for fourteen years. Maurice has made famous his restaurant, Maurice's, which is well known for its excellent gourmet cuisine. Maurice is from Normandy, France, where he lived for twenty years. He remembers Christmas to be "mostly for children. It was a real family affair with lots of wonderful things to eat!"

Maurice was kind enough to divulge his traditional Christmas Log recipe.

Maurice Thuillier
CHRISTMAS LOG

SPONGE CAKE

10 egg yolks
½ cup sugar
½ cup flour
10 egg whites

Mix the yolks and sugar together until stiff. In separate bowl, beat the whites until stiff. Fold the two together along with flour. Bake at 350° for about 10 minutes on a greased and floured flat pan. Let cool 10 minutes, then roll it up and cover with a damp napkin.

BUTTER CREAM

8 egg yolks
¼ cup sugar
1½ cups milk

Bring the milk to a boil. In a separate sauce pan, mix the yolks and sugar. Add the milk and bring it almost to a boil. Let cool. Then add 1 pound soft sweet butter. Divide butter cream into 3 portions. Flavor each individually—1 chocolate, 1 coffee, 1 vanilla.

Unroll log and frost with chocolate or coffee. Reroll and frost and decorate outside. Use a fork to make texture in the log. Vanilla frosting can be colored to make holly.

To make the mushrooms to decorate, beat leftover egg whites until stiff. Fold in ½ cup powdered sugar and ½ cup sugar. Add a little lemon juice. Shape into mushrooms and dry overnight.
Serves 10

CHESTNUT STUFFING

Many serve turkey as their Christmas dinner. Maurice has a wonderful recipe for chestnut stuffing that we've tried and agree it's the best we've ever had.

2 cups chestnuts
¼ cup onions
butter
½ cup celery
chicken broth
salt, pepper
bay leaf
gizzards and liver
1 apple (sliced and skinned)
¼ cup currants
basil
bread crumbs

Peel the chestnuts with a paring knife.

Dip them in boiling water for 8 to 10 seconds, then remove the skins.

Slice the onions and saute in butter. Add the celery—cover and simmer.

Add the chestnuts and cover with chicken broth. Add a bay leaf, salt and pepper.

Gradually add raw gizzards and liver, apple, currants, and basil.

Soak bread crumbs in milk. Add chestnut mixture to soaked bread crumbs, toss and stuff into turkey cavity.

THE BURTONS

Bill and Gale Burton came to Aspen in the '60s. Packing up their six youngsters, they left the midwest with a dream in mind. For six years, they ran the Heatherbed Lodge along with the Williams family. Since that time, they have gotten away from the lodging business and have found more time to spend Christmas together as a family. On Christmas Day, the family convenes for a traditional dinner where each of the children—Tab, Diana, Shane, Shannon, Bruce and Michelle—contribute their own dish to the meal.

Gale has a unique recipe for a bread that she molds into the shapes of a lion and several small lambs. □

Gale Burton
PEACEABLE BREAD
"The Lamb and The Lion"

BASIC BREAD RECIPE

1 package yeast
2 cups warm water
3 tablespoons honey
2 teaspoons salt
¼ cup oil
7 cups flour

Start yeast in warm water with honey. Let stand 5 minutes. Add salt, oil and flour a little at a time until you can work dough with your hands. If sticky, add more flour, knead and make sculpture on cookie sheet or foil. The dough sculpture must lie flat, not standing. Stick the various pieces together with a little water. Parts will grow together as the dough rises. Let rise 10 to 20 minutes.

Bake at 350° for 20 to 30 minutes, depending on size of figure. Remember not to make the sculpture bigger than your oven!

1. Divide dough into one big ball and 6 medium-size balls.

2. Flatten the big ball—sort of square for body (place it as shown).

3. Form backwards "L" shape for back leg out of one of the medium balls.

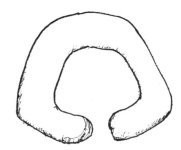

4. Flatten another ball and form a horseshoe shape for the arms of the lion.

5. Form rounded-off triangle shape for head.

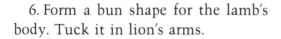

6. Form a bun shape for the lamb's body. Tuck it in lion's arms.

7. Make a small ball for lamb's head and ears.

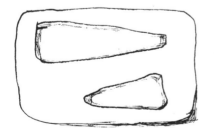

8. Cut or form the two noses from a flattened piece of dough (use a dab of water for glue).

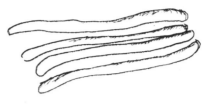

9. Roll all the rest of the dough into snakes for the mane and lamb's curls.

10. Save three long snakes for the braided or twisted lion's tail.

11. Use raisins for eyes.

12. Poke fork prongs into body of lion, as air holes and decoration (so he won't split open).

13. Whip up a raw egg and paint your beasts all over, gently.

14. Let rise 10 minutes and bake at 350° for about 45 minutes, depending on size. Then eat!

THE SARDYS

Tom and Alice Rachel moved to Aspen in 1938 from Monte Vista. Since that time, they have spent most of their years in the beautiful brick Victorian on Main Street. Each year at Christmastime, they would decorate their blue spruce with lights. The first year, Tom used a step ladder, and as time went by, they came to need assistance from the City cherry picker. Now, the tree has grown so tall that they can no longer decorate it.

Alice Rachel has given us her mother's recipe for Funnel Cakes and her own favorite Mincemeat Bars. □

MINCE PIES

The custom behind mince pies at Christmas dates back several centuries. The most famous pie in the history of Christmas folklore was one which was prepared for Sir Henry Grey in London in 1770. Being nine feet in circumference, it weighed so much that it had to be wheeled into the dining hall. Baked inside of it were four geese, four wild ducks, two woodcocks, two turkeys, four partridges, seven blackbirds, six pigeons, two rabbits, two neat's tongues, two bushels of flour, twenty pounds of butter, and various spices and vegetables. Some Englishmen have been heard to say, "The Devil himself dare not appear in Cornwall during Christmas for fear of being baked in a pie." □

Alice Rachel Sardy
MINCEMEAT BARS

2½ cups all-purpose flour
  ½ teaspoon cinnamon
  ¼ teaspoon salt
  ¾ cup butter or margarine
  ¾ cup sugar
  1 egg, unbeaten (reserve 1 tablespoon egg white)
1½ cups mincemeat
Sift dry ingredients.

Cream butter, add sugar and cream well. Blend in unbeaten egg and almond extract. Add dry ingredients.

Roll out half of dough on greased baking sheet. Spread with mincemeat.

Roll out remaining dough between waxed paper and invert on mincemeat.

Brush with egg white, slightly beaten. Bake at 350° for about 30 minutes.
Sprinkle with ½ cup chopped almonds.

Alice Rachel Sardy
FUNNEL CAKES
"Carpet Rags"

---

3 eggs
1 quart milk
salt enough to season
flour to make a batter that will run
    through a funnel

Have a kettle with plenty of hot fat. Fill a funnel half full of the batter, and run it around from side to side in the fat and fry a delicate brown.

This recipe was given to me by my mother, Osa Peck, who had it when she was married in 1900.

THE LITTLES

Bill and Ruth Little moved to Aspen from Seattle, Washington, nineteen years ago. They have owned and run the popular Little Cliff's Bakery ever since their arrival.

The Littles have delighted the town with their "doughnut tree," which is located directly outside of their bakery. It started years ago as a Christmas gift to the birds. Now one can see it anytime throughout the year.

Many may remember the Littles' "Cinnamon Bear" contest they held every year around Christmas.

The "Cinnamon Bear" is a story about two children, Judy and Jimmy. One night, while decorating their tree with their family, they go to the attic to look for the silver star that belongs on the tree. Not finding it, they fall asleep and their dreams become the search for the silver star. They meet the Cinnamon Bear who leads them on incredible adventures, flying them through strange and distant lands. Their last hope is Santa Claus, who has the star in his bag. The children hear their mother calling them for dinner. They awaken to find the silver star and the Cinnamon Bear lying next to them. They run downstairs to put the star and the bear on the tree. Then they wonder if it had all been a dream, or if it really happened. They knew it was true when the Cinnamon Bear winked at Judy and Jimmy from the tree.

The contest involved the children in Aspen listening to the "Cinnamon Bear" story which was heard nightly on a local radio station. When the entire story was told, the children did their own interpretations of the story. Bill remembers, "The children loved the story so much. They all were so creative and did such a good job that it was extremely difficult to judge the winners." □

Bill Little

ANGEL KISSES

1 cup soft butter
½ cup confectioners sugar
2 tablespoons vanilla
2 cups sifted flour
½ teaspoon salt
2 cups ground walnuts

Mix together well; roll into small 1-inch balls and bake at 300° for about 15 minutes. Test for doneness.

When they're still warm, sprinkle with powdered sugar!

Makes 4 dozen.

Bill Little

DATE BARS

1 cup confectioners sugar
1 tablespoon oil
2 eggs, beaten
¼ cup cake flour
¼ teaspoon salt
½ teaspoon baking powder
¾ cup chopped filberts
1 cup chopped dates
1 teaspoon vanilla

Add sugar and melted oil to eggs, and blend well; add sifted dry ingredients, filberts, dates, and vanilla.

Pour into greased 9"×9" pan.

Bake at 350° for 25 minutes. Cut into bars and roll in confectioners sugar.

THE RITSCH FAMILY

Dorle moved to Aspen from Bodensee, Germany, in 1964. She met Ludwig at a T-Lazy-7 Ranch chuckwagon dinner, and they were married two years later. Ludwig is originally from Arosa, Switzerland.

The Ritsches, who have two children—Markus and Daniel—follow Dorle's German traditions in celebrating Christmas.

Dorle taught the art of making dough ornaments at Colorado Mountain College for several years. She has shared with us these recipes and her directions for making her "Little Dough People." □

Dorle Ritsch

LITTLE DOUGH PEOPLE FOR MY CHRISTMAS TREE

Every year I try to make some new handmade crafts for each of our boys and for the Christmas tree.

RECIPE FOR DOUGH ORNAMENTS

2 cups any cheap flour
1 cup water (more or less)
1 cup salt
2 tablespoons oil
Knead everything for approximately 5 minutes. Dough should be rather sticky and tough.

UTENSILS

You must have a few essentials ready before you start.

Eggwash—for attaching pieces together.

Brush, toothpicks, cookie sheet and a garlic press (for making hair).

Now you start making your head. Roll a little dough ball in your hands. Put on a cookie sheet.

Try to shape a body. Brush both pieces with eggwash where they touch. Roll two little oblong pieces for arms. Watch out—don't make the body too large. It looks better and cuter if the head is at least as large as the body.

Now I start to shape "chaps." Shape a little belt and buckle, of course. Every real cowboy has a good-looking buckle! You can get carried away decorating him—give him a holster and gun, etc.

All right, look at your creation—what is missing? Of course, he does not have any hair yet, nor does he have a face.

59

Start rolling a very tiny little ball in your index finger and thumb for his nose. "Glue" it on with eggwash. With your toothpick, poke two holes on either side of nose for eyes. Now, eggwash his whole head. Fill your garlic press with dough and start squeezing out some spaghetti. It is all up to you. He can be either bushy or clean-cut, curly or long and stringy—your imagination can go wild!

His hat is rather tricky. I usually form a flat piece like a pancake with both my thumbs and index fingers. Bring it up—make it real fluffy and high. Do not be afraid, the second one will turn out better (put in a little florist wire hook before the baking process).

I give him a hatband and, of course, he needs a feather in his hat. Poke a hole with your toothpick and leave the pick in during the baking process. Twist it several times so toothpick does not get baked in. The feather, of course, is glued in after the little guy is all finished and out of the oven.

Remove toothpick immediately.

You can either leave him natural or paint some important details, but I do not suggest painting the whole ornament, since I like the effect of the dough.

I usually shellac my ornaments with either Bullseye Zinsser Shellac, orange, or with Polimer High-gloss Resin finish, which is rather expensive.

Before shellacking, I take a few felt-tip pens and paint a few freckles on and around his nose.

Good luck. This is a fun project for all ages.

Dorle Ritsch

SWISS WALNUT LECKERLI

1 cup ground walnuts (about ¼ pound)
1 cup ground almonds (about ¼ pound)
½ cup flour
3 tablespoons superfine sugar
1 tablespoon grated orange rind
¼ teaspoon ground allspice
¼ teaspoon ground mace or nutmeg
¼ teaspoon ground cinnamon
½ cup chopped citron
1 egg white, stiffly beaten
1 tablespoon honey
1 tablespoon Grand Marnier or Cognac

GLAZE

2 tablespoons confectioners sugar
1 tablespoon water
1 tablespoon Grand Marnier or Cognac
Preheat oven to 425°.

Combine ground nuts, flour, sugar, orange rind, spices, chopped citron and egg white. Heat honey with the Grand Marnier and add it. Blend well with the hands.

Shape batter into a rectangle about 3"×12". Cut into fingers about ¾" thick. Place the fingers, or *leckerli*, on an oiled baking sheet and bake for ½ hour.

For the glaze, combine sugar, water and Grand Marnier. Brush mixture over fingers and let dry.

Makes about 16 cookies

Dorle Ritsch

TRÜFFEL

"Rum Balls"

This is more like a candy but not really for the kids.

¾ cup butter
1 cup powdered sugar
8 ounces German sweet chocolate
4 ounces bittersweet chocolate
1 cup raisins, soaked in rum overnight
Whip butter until fluffy; add powdered sugar.

In double boiler, melt both kinds of chocolate. Add to butter mixture; add raisins soaked in rum, mix until all ingredients are evenly mixed in. Cool in refrigerator approximately 40 minutes. Form little balls and roll in chocolate decorations. (It works better if you rinse your hands constantly in ice-cold water.)

Cool Trüffel and store in airtight container in your refrigerator.

Dorle Ritsch

MARZIPAN CHRISTMAS COOKIES

2¾ cups unbleached flour
1 teaspoon ground cardamom
¼ teaspoon baking soda
1 cup butter or margarine
1 cup light brown sugar
¼ cup sour cream
½ cup chopped, blanched almonds
2 egg whites
1 can, or 8-ounce package, almond paste
1 cup granulated sugar
cherry or strawberry preserves

Sift flour with cardamom, baking soda and salt. Set aside.

In large bowl, let butter stand at room temperature until softened. With electric mixer at medium speed, beat butter, brown sugar and sour cream until fluffy.

At low speed, beat in flour mixture until combined. Stir in the chopped, blanched almonds.

Turn out dough onto lightly floured surface; divide in half. Shape each half into a roll 1½" in diameter. Wrap in waxed paper or plastic wrap. Refrigerate until firm—about 6 hours or overnight.

THE GUYS

Peter and Barbara moved to Aspen in 1960 from Massachusetts. They have owned and run The Steak Pit restaurant since that time. They have raised two sons, Charlie and Cary, both of whom raced for the Aspen Ski Club.

Peter and Barbara are both very active in the community and have donated much time and energy to Aspen's various organizations. Peter has served for over twelve years on the Aspen School Board and is the chairman of the County Planning and Zoning Commission. Barbara has worked for the Thrift Shop, the Community Church, the Aspen Ski Club, and the Aspen Yacht Club. She delights her Steak Pit employees by cooking them creative and delicious meals.

Barbara shares with us her Federal Cake, which is an old family recipe that she makes every year and gives out as Christmas gifts. Also tempting are her recipes for Cape Cod Pudding and Persimmon Pudding. □

Christmas Cake Folklore

Pies and cakes have been a traditional part of the Christmas feast since the Middle Ages. Originally, these delicacies were made with a flour which was supposed to have a mystic significance, and in most places they were sampled by everyone who entered the home on Christmas Day. Sometimes a cake would be baked for each member of the family and it was assumed that those whose cakes were cracked were marked for bad luck or even death. □

Grandmother Guy
FEDERAL CAKE

1 lb. butter
1 lb. sugar (2 cups)
1 lb. flour (3 cups)
½ lb. cut-up golden raisins or currants
5 eggs
½ pint sour cream
1 wine glass brandy (at least 4 oz.)
1½ tsp. nutmeg
1 tsp. soda

Preheat oven to 325°. Cream the butter, slowly add the sugar and beat until light. Add the eggs, one at a time, beating each in well. Mix the flour, soda and nutmeg together and add to this mixture, alternately in three parts with the sour cream, stirring until well blended. Add raisins or currants and mix well. Spoon into three small buttered and floured pans. Use fancy ornamental pans or molds. Bake at 325° for 1 hour. If using one loaf pan, bake for 1¼-1½ hours, or until a toothpick comes out clean. Cool in the pan for 5 minutes before turning out onto a rack.

Grandmother Guy
CAPE COD PUDDING

1 package gingerbread mix
   (Dromedary brand is the best)
3 Tbs. grated orange rind
¼ cup raisins
½ cup chopped nuts
¼ cup orange juice
1 cup cold water

Preheat oven to 350°.

To gingerbread mix, add orange rind, raisins and nuts, mixing thoroughly. Then to this mixture, add orange juice and water, stirring very well. Pour batter into a greased 8" square pan. Bake in 350° oven for 30 to 35 minutes. Cool pudding, cut into squares and serve with any fruit sauces, custard or lemon sauce, or whipped cream. *Serves 8*

Barbara Guy
PERSIMMON PUDDING

1 cup sugar
1 cup flour
1 cup mashed persimmon pulp
(about 3 persimmons)
2 tsp. soda
⅛ tsp. salt
1 beaten egg
½ cup milk
1 Tbs. melted butter
1 tsp. cinnamon
½ cup nuts
½ cup raisins

Preheat oven to 350°. Combine all ingredients and mix well. Pour into greased and floured pan and bake for 1 hour at 350°.

Serve with lemon sauce.

LEMON SAUCE

½ cup sugar
1 Tbs. cornstarch
1 cup boiling water
2 Tbs. butter
2 Tbs. lemon juice
lemon rind—grated, about 1 Tbs.
freshly grated nutmeg
pinch of salt

Mix sugar and cornstarch together in a saucepan. Add boiling water, stirring constantly. Bring to a boil and boil 5 minutes. Remove from stove and add butter, lemon juice, lemon rind, nutmeg and salt. Stir well and serve over pudding while still warm.

THE GUNS'

The Guns family—Leo, Margaret, Lilly and Irene—originate in Holland and have been living in Aspen for several years.

Margaret has given us her recipe for *Advocaat*, a traditional Dutch Christmas cheer.

Lilly and I used to make her recipe for *Speculaas* every year at Christmas. Her grandfather was famous for his pastry shop in Holland. □

Margaret Guns
ADVOCAAT
(A traditional Christmas cheer)

Beat until thick, with mixer:
10 eggs
½ teaspoon salt
1¼ cup sugar
Add slowly, always beating:
 2 cups brandy
1½ teaspoon vanilla

Pour the mixture into double boiler or heavy saucepan. Beat over low heat with wire whisk until warm—not hot —and thickened. Remove from heat and stir in vanilla. It is served in a glass and eaten with a spoon. Top with whipped cream!

Margaret Guns
SPECULAAS

3 cups flour
1 cup soft butter
1 cup brown sugar
2 tsp. baking powder
¼ tsp. salt
2 Tbs. milk
1 tsp. cinnamon
½ tsp. nutmeg
¼ tsp. ground cloves
½ cup slivered almonds
2 packages almond paste

Knead all ingredients into a small ball. Save a few almonds for decorations. Roll out half of dough into ¼ inch thick. Place on buttered baking sheet. Spread with a layer of almond paste and top with second half of dough. Bake 40 minutes at 400°.

Cool and decorate with almonds.

O P A L   M A R O L T

Opal was born in Aspen and her family has lived in the valley for many years. She is of Swedish origin and has given us her recipe for Swedish Spritz Cookies. □

Opal Marolt
SWEDISH SPRITZ COOKIES

1 pound butter
3 egg yolks
1½ cups sugar
1 teaspoon vanilla
¼ teaspoon almond extract
4 cups flour

Cream butter. Add vanilla and almond extract. Add sugar gradually. Add egg yolks one at a time, beating well after each addition. Add enough flour until it is right to handle.
Bake at 375° until golden.

THE NOSTDAHLS

Connie and Magne Nostdahl have lived in Aspen since 1958. Connie has run the Scandinavian Design shop for sixteen years, and Magne, who is originally from Bergen, Norway, is a ski instructor and contractor. They have three children—Karin, Svein and Kristin. She has given us two traditional Norwegian recipes.

□

Connie Nostdahl
SILLSALLAD
(Herring Salad in Sour Cream Sauce)

1 cup finely chopped herring
   (salt, matjes, pickled, Bismarck)
½ pound finely chopped cooked tongue
   or veal (optional)
½ cup finely chopped cold boiled
   potatoes
3 cups finely chopped cold beets,
   freshly cooked or canned
½ cup finely chopped apple, cored and
   peeled
¼ cup finely chopped onion
½ cup finely chopped dill pickle

4 tablespoons finely chopped fresh dill
2 tablespoons white wine vinegar
salt
freshly ground black pepper

In a large mixing bowl, combine the finely chopped herring, optional meat, potatoes, beets, apple, onion, and pickle. Mix 3 tablespoons of the dill with the vinegar, and add salt and pepper to taste. Pour over the salad ingredients and toss gently with a wooden spoon.

66

DRESSING

3 chilled hard-cooked eggs
1 tablespoon prepared mustard
2 tablespoons white wine vinegar
¼ cup vegetable oil
2-4 tablespoons heavy cream

Remove the yolks from the hard-cooked eggs. Mince the whites and set them aside. Force the yolks through a sieve into a small bowl with the back of a large spoon, then mash them to a paste with the tablespoon of prepared mustard. Gradually beat in the vinegar and oil, then the cream, a tablespoon at a time, until the sauce has the consistency of heavy cream. Pour over the salad, mix lightly but thoroughly, cover, and chill for at least 2 hours.

Just before serving, transfer the salad to a large serving bowl or platter and sprinkle it with the minced egg whites and the remaining chopped dill.

SAUCE

1 cup sour cream
3 tablespoons beet juice
½ teaspoon lemon juice

Stir the beet and lemon juice into the sour cream until it is smooth and well blended. Pass this sauce separately.
To serve 8 to 10

Connie Nostdahl
KRUMKAKE

1 cup butter
1 cup sugar
4 eggs
1 teaspoon grated lemon rind
½ teaspoon cinnamon
2 egg yolks
2 cups flour
1 cup whipping cream
½ teaspoon crushed cardamom

Cook, using a *krumkake* iron (which you can purchase at any kitchen store). Roll onto a wooden spoon handle to make it cone-shaped.

Rather than baking, cook on top of the stove in the iron. Instructions for cooking will come with the *krumkake* iron.

THE UHLS

Sepp and Gretl Uhl moved to Aspen from Garmisch in 1953. Gretl spent her formative years in the Olympic Village of Garmisch where her parents ran a restaurant called Hartl's. She kept busy skiing on the German National Ski Team for eleven years.

Sepp and Gretl both instructed for the Aspen Skiing Corporation when they first moved to Aspen.

In December, 1966, Gretl's world-famous restaurant on Aspen Mountain began. She ran her small mountain restaurant until 1980, serving only the best homemade foods. No one will forget her soups, and, of course, her *strudel.* Many a beginner has tackled Aspen Mountain just for a piece of warm *strudel* topped with homemade whipped cream.

She has given us two of her favorite German Christmas cookie recipes. □

Gretl Uhl
SPITZBUBEN

2½ sticks butter
1 cup sugar
2 eggs
4 cups flour
1 cup ground almonds

Mix all ingredients together and knead the dough. Roll out to ¼" thickness. Cut out with circular or star-shaped cutter. Cut out an additional smaller circle in the center of one half of the cookies. Spread one half of the cookies with jam after they have baked and top with second half of cookies. Roll in powdered sugar.

Bake at 350° for 10 minutes.

Gretl Uhl
CINNAMON STARS

3 egg whites
2 cups powdered sugar
1 teaspoon vanilla extract
few drops almond extract
1 teaspoon cinnamon
2½ cups ground hazelnuts or almonds

Beat egg whites until stiff; add powdered sugar gradually. From this, set aside 2 heaping tablespoons. Add rest of ingredients.

Carefully knead dough on board. Use ground nuts instead of flour to work on. Roll out to ¼" thick.

Dip star cutter in powdered sugar and cut out cookies. Grease the cookie sheet, cover with waxed paper, and grease the waxed paper.

Brush the cookies with egg whites that were set aside and bake at 325×for 35 minutes.

Jan Wirth
HERB SALTS
see THE WIRTHS *on page 13*

THYME SALT *Makes ½ cup each*

Up to one month ahead, with mortar and pestle, crush 3 tablespoons thyme leaves to a fine powder. In a small bowl with a fork, mix together thyme and ½ cup salt. Store in tightly covered container.

OREGANO SALT

Same as above, but use 3 tablespoons of oregano leaves.

TARRAGON SALT

Same as above, but use 2 tablespoons of tarragon leaves.

Jan Wirth
ALL-SEASONS VINEGAR
(Makes 1 quart)

¼ cup +
 1 tablespoon crumbled, dried
  marjoram leaves
¼ cup crumbled, dried mint leaves
 2 tablespoons crumbled, dried basil
  leaves
 2 tablespoons crumbled, dried
  tarragon leaves
 1 tablespoon crumbled, dried
  rosemary leaves
½ teaspoon crushed dill seed
¼ teaspoon black pepper
⅛ teaspoon whole allspice

⅛ teaspoon ground cloves
 1 quart cider vinegar

Place all ingredients in clean quart jar or crock; cover. Let stand in cool place 3 weeks. Stir and crush herbs and spices daily with a wooden spoon.

Strain vinegar through filter paper into clean bottles; seal.

CHRISTMAS STOLLEN
see THE STAPLETONS *on page 20*

6 cups flour
1 cup milk
¾ cup melted butter
3 eggs
½ pound seedless raisins
½ pound currants
½ cup sugar
¼ teaspoon mace
½ teaspoon grated lemon peel
1 tablespoon lemon juice
½ tablespoon cognac or rum
¼ pound chopped almonds
½ teaspoon salt
2 packages yeast, undissolved in ¼ cup
   warm water
¼ teaspoon grated nutmeg

Sift flour into large bowl, add milk, melted butter and eggs until mixed. Add rest of ingredients. Work the dough with hands. Dough should be stiff. Beat and fold dough repeatedly until smooth. Cover bowl lightly with towel. Let stand in warm place for six hours or until it rises to double in bulk.

Shape into loaves with slightly pointed ends. Place in greased baking pan or put two loaves on a cookie sheet.

Bake at 350° for one hour. Spread with melted butter and sprinkle with powdered sugar.

Here is the Maces' Christmas dinner menu:
see THE MACES *on page 24*

Wild mushroom soup

Salad and sourdough bread

Goose—served with their seven grains
(a combination of different grains sauteed and baked in a broth in the oven)
and vegetables à la Toklat

Fruit with blackberry sauce
for dessert

Homemade tea

Isabel has kindly contributed the following goose recipe.

Isabel Mace
RECIPE FOR COOKING GOOSE

You must prepare a goose properly because it is a very fatty bird. Isabel suggests cooking it the day before.

Roast the goose in fruit juices: bing cherry, boysenberry, blackberry or chokecherry in a 350° oven and baste it while cooking.

When done, remove the juices and set out to cool. Also, cool the goose.

The next day, remove the hardened fat from the top of the cold juices. The cold juices will be gelled, so heat them until they're liquid once again. Then put the sliced goose into the juices to marinate for a few hours at room temperature. Before serving, heat the goose slices in order to serve hot.

Mary Eshbaugh Hayes
SUGAR COOKIES
see THE HAYESES *on page 26*

1 cup shortening
1 cup sugar
2 eggs
½ teaspoon salt
1½ teaspoon vanilla
2½ cups flour
1 teaspoon baking powder

Cream sugar and shortening, add eggs, then rest of ingredients. Chill. Roll out and cut with fancy cookie cutters.

Frost with different colors of confectioners sugar frosting—made with box of confectioners sugar, butter the size of a walnut, vanilla, cream or milk to spreading consistency. Dust with sugar. These make the best Christmas cookies, or special cookies for any occasion.

Recipe from her book Aspen Potpourri

Mary Eshbaugh Hayes
GREAT-GRANPA'S TAFFY

2 cups white sugar
1 cup brown Karo syrup
2 tablespoons vinegar
2 tablespoons butter

Boil until it will crack in water. Add ½ teaspoon soda. Pour on buttered plat-

ter. When cool, pull until light-colored and cut with shears.

Cut small squares of waxed paper and wrap individual pieces of taffy—twist ends of paper.

Put into gaily painted coffee cans.

Hjördis Skaeringsson
MARINATED HERRING
see THE SKAERINGSSONS *on page 27*

Buy salted herring.

Put in a large bowl of cold water and leave for a day. Keep changing the water and keep it fresh.

After the day is up, if the fish is still salty, place in a bowl of milk for ½ hour.

Fillet the herring and cut into small pieces.

Marinate:
  3 cups water
  1½ cups sugar
  1½ cups vinegar

Bring above ingredients to boil in saucepan.

Slice 2 red onions.

Slice 4 carrots.

Put everything in a large glass jar and leave in the refrigerator. The longer it sits, the better it is!

Hjördis Skaeringsson
RED CABBAGE

---

  1 medium head red cabbage
  5 cooking apples
  2 tablespoons sugar
  3 tablespoons California red wine
      vinegar
  1 tablespoon butter
1¼ teaspoons salt
  ½ teaspoon pepper
  ¼ cup red dinner wine

Shred the cabbage finely. Core and cut the apples in small pieces. Combine with sugar the vinegar, butter, salt, and pepper in a saucepan. Cook slowly, covered, for 45 minutes to an hour or until soft. Stir often. Add the wine for the last 10 minutes of cooking.

Hjördis Skaeringsson
JÓLAKAKA
(Icelandic Christmas cake)

2 cups flour
1½ teaspoon baking powder
½-1 teaspoon cardamom
1 cup sugar
½ cup butter
½ cup milk
2 eggs
½ cup raisins
1 cup candied fruits of lemon, orange, cherry, and pineapple

Heat the oven to 350°.

Mix ingredients together and place in a greased bread pan. Bake for an hour.

Wassail

Before giving you Sigrid Stapleton's recipe for her delicious *Wassail* bowl, we thought you might be interested in knowing the origin of this drink.

Today, Christmas wassailing is not practiced. However, in years past, wassailing was a very important part of agricultural ritual. In England, these rituals focused on the apple orchards. The people felt if they saluted the trees in the midwinter, it would insure them a crop for the coming year. The brew that they used was mulled cider or ale with roasted apples and perhaps an egg in it. The wassail procession visited the major orchards of the parish and caroled along the way. Major trees were selected in each orchard, and the roots were sprinkled with the liquor. Sometimes, a bowl of the liquor was broken against the trunk like champagne bottles against a ship.

Great noise was made to terrorize evil spirits away by firing a gun, shouting, or blowing on a bullhorn. The procession usually danced around an honored tree to insure good luck. The care with which the ceremony had been executed was measured by the size and health of the crop for the coming year.

Much attention is now paid to the carrying in of the great bowl, the singing of a song praising the drink and the ritual of crowding around for a taste of the festive drink.

73

Sigrid Stapleton
WASSAIL BOWL
see THE STAPLETONS *on page 20*

In a saucepan, bring 4 cups of apple cider to a boil over moderate heat, add ½ cup firmly packed dark brown sugar. Cook the mixture, stirring until the sugar is dissolved. Remove the pan from the heat and add ½ cup dark rum, ¼ cup brandy, 1 tablespoon orange flavored liqueur, ¼ teaspoon each of cinnamon and ground cloves, ⅛ teaspoon ground allspice, salt to taste, and ½ lemon and ½ orange, thinly sliced. Heat the mixture over moderate heat, stirring for 2 minutes. Pour the wassail into wine glasses and top it with whipped cream and freshly grated nutmeg.

Serves 6

Sigrid Stapleton
ANISE DROP COOKIES

Preheat oven to 325°.

Sift 1 cup of sugar. Beat 3 eggs until light. Add the sugar gradually. Beat with an electric mixer for 3-5 minutes on medium speed. Add ½ teaspoon vanilla.

Sift, before measuring, 2 cups all-purpose flour. Resift with 1 teaspoon double-acting baking powder.

Add 1½ tablespoons crushed anise seed. Beat the batter for 5 minutes.

Drop ½ teaspoon at a time, well apart, on a cookie sheet lined with foil.

The dough should flatten to one inch round. Permit the drops to dry at room temperature for 18 hours. Bake the cookies until they begin to color, about 12 minutes. When done, they will have a puffed, meringue-like top on a soft cookie base.

Makes 96 1" cookies

Louiva Stapleton, David's mother,
grew up in the Stallard House in Aspen that is now the Historical Society Museum.
She has given us her recipes for Oyster Stew and Potica.

Louiva Stapleton
POTICA
(A Yugoslavian bread)

Prepare a sweet bread dough and roll it out thin. Spread melted butter over the dough. Then add a mixture of one egg, nutmeg, cinnamon and sugar, and spread on top of the dough.

Add nuts and raisins.

Roll up the dough to form a long loaf. Take one end and roll inward to form a circle.

Let it rise again.

Bake at 350° for an hour.

Louiva Stapleton
OYSTER STEW

Slowly heat 2-3 quarts of milk, but do not boil. Boil 1 quart of oysters in their own juices until done.

Add a stick of butter, salt, pepper, cayenne, and Worcestershire sauce to milk, then add the cooked oysters.

Just before serving, grind up saltines or oyster crackers, and serve on top of the stew.

Lynne Wille
FRUITCAKE
see THE WILLES on page 29

8 cups flour
5 sticks unsalted butter
1 cup brown sugar
12 eggs
6 cups fruitcake mix
2 cups yellow raisins
½ teaspoon soda
1 teaspoon baking powder
1 cup strong coffee
¼ cup honey
1 cup currants

½ cup sherry wine
1 tablespoon rum flavoring
1 cup orange marmalade
2 teaspoons cinnamon
3 cups nuts
2 cups small gumdrops, chopped

Line pans with waxed paper. Put pan with water in bottom of oven. Bake at 250° for 3 hours. Wrap in wine-soaked cloth and foil. Store 1 month.

Makes about 10 cakes of all sizes

Marsha Brendlinger
GINGERBREAD MEN
see THE BRENDLINGERS *on page 22*

4 cups sifted cake flour
2½ teaspoons baking powder
½ teaspoon salt
¾ cup soft shortening
1 cup honey
½ cup sugar
2 unbeaten eggs
1 teaspoon vanilla
4 teaspoons milk

Sift the dry ingredients. Mix the shortening with the sugar, eggs and vanilla. Bake at 325° for 10 to 12 minutes, or until well done.
Use a gingerbread man cookie cutter to shape the cookies, and use colored icing to decorate these gingerbread men.

Marsha Brendlinger
CREAMY RAISIN RICE PUDDING

1 cup seedless raisins
1 cup cooked rice

Place the raisins and rice in a greased dish.

3 cups milk
1 tablespoon butter

Heat the milk and butter until scalding.

3 eggs
½ cup sugar

1 teaspoon vanilla
¼ teaspoon nutmeg

Lightly beat these 4 ingredients together and gradually stir into the heated milk. Pour over the raisin and rice mixture. Sprinkle with nutmeg. Set in a shallow pan of water.

Bake at 350° until done, about 1 hour.

Karen Batista
APPLESAUCE COFFEE SPICE DROPS
see KAREN BATISTA *on page 39*

Mix together thoroughly:
 1 cup soft butter
 2 cups brown sugar (or 1½ cups fine)

2 eggs
½ cup cold coffee
3½ cups unbleached white flour

1 teaspoon each soda, salt,
    cinnamon, cloves
2 cups applesauce
1 cup raisins (cut up if you have
    patience—I don't)
½ cup chopped nuts

Bake at 400° 9-15 minutes until light
brown—really like a cake in cookie
form—good!

Karen Batista

ITALIAN COOKIES

6 cups unbleached white flour
1½ cups sugar
6 teaspoons baking powder
    (3 teaspoons high-altitude)
6 eggs
1 teaspoon vanilla
    pinch salt
2 teaspoons anise flavoring
½ pound butter or oleo
½ cup almonds (sliced raw—optional)

Grease cookie sheet.

Cream butter, add sugar, eggs, and dry
ingredients.

Grease hands, shape quickly into 2 or 3
logs (3 is best).

Bake 20-25 minutes at 375° or until
baked through.

Slice on a slant and brown under
broiler (toast) until light brown on the
edges.

THE MELVILLES

Ralph and Marian Melville met and were married in Aspen twenty-five years ago. Since that time, they have been successful both in establishing their homey Mountain Chalet ski lodge, and in raising a large, closely knit family. Their six children—Julie, Frank, Nancy, Susan, Karen and Craig, plus one whom they have taken under their wing, Riley Pond—usually had to remain patient until January. Then, when things slowed down a bit, they were finally able to open their presents. Christmas time in the Mountain Chalet was spent with employees and guests, many of whom return year after year. This past Christmas, they celebrated the Mountain Chalet's 25th anniversary. Each year, they would have a large potluck Christmas dinner where all could take part in the custom of giving.

Marian would prepare the turkey and her special cranberry mold, and Ralph would make his famous stuffing.

Now that the children are older, the Melvilles are more concerned with getting away from the material side of Christmas, and returning to the truer meaning. Gifts are still exchanged, but on a smaller scale, and a warm religious feeling prevails.

Marian Melville
CRANBERRY MOLD

2 cups ground cranberries
2 cups sugar
2 packages lemon Jello
4 cups warm water
1 cup diced celery
1 cup broken walnuts
1 ground-up orange

Combine cranberries and sugar, and let stand.

Dissolve lemon Jello in warm water and chill until partially solid. Add the rest of the ingredients, and chill until firm.

Use a round mold.

Mix ½ cup of mayonnaise and ½ cup of whipped cream, and place in the middle of the mold.

Make this mold a day in advance.

Serves 10-12

Anneke DePagter
OLIEBOLLEN
see THE DE PAGTERS *on page 30*

Anneke loves to make *Oliebollen*, a Dutch doughnut-like ball filled with fruit and traditionally served on New Year's Eve.

1 envelope active dry yeast
¼ cup warm water
   sugar
3 tablespoons butter
1 cup milk, scalded
2 teaspoons salt

2 eggs, beaten
5 cups (about) all-purpose flour
¾ cup raisins
¾ cup currants
¾ cup diced citron
fat for frying

Soften yeast in the water with 1 tablespoon sugar. Add butter to hot milk, cool to lukewarm, and add dissolved yeast. Stir in ¾ cup sugar, salt and eggs.

Gradually add enough flour to make a soft dough. Add raisins, currants and citron and mix well. Knead on lightly floured board for about 6 minutes, or until smooth and satiny. Put in greased bowl and turn to bring greased side up. Cover and let rise until double in bulk. Heat fat (365° on a frying thermometer). With two tablespoons dipped in fat, spoon off pieces of dough and form balls of about 1¾". Carefully drop the balls in hot fat and fry until golden brown. Drain on paper towels and serve heaped in a bowl and sprinkled with plenty of powdered sugar.

Anne Vitte Morse
AEBLESKIVER
see THE MORSES *on page 14*
("Apple slices"—they taste like pancakes)

---

2 cups milk
2 eggs
1 package yeast
1 tablespoon sugar
1 teaspoon salt
2¼ cups flour
2/3 stick butter

You need to use an *Aebleskiver* pan. You can find one in a kitchen shop or a hardware store.

Warm the milk until it is lukewarm. Mix in the yeast and butter, stir until the butter is almost melted. Mix in eggs, sugar, salt, and flour. Let dough stand for about half an hour.

Warm up the *Aebleskiver* pan and put a small amount of melted butter into each hole. Put in dough about halfway, cook under medium heat. Use a knitting needle to turn the *Aebleskiver* when they are brown on one side. Make sure they are cooked all the way through. When an *Aebleskiver* is done, it should resemble a round ball. Eat with raspberry jam, sugar or honey.

Velbekomme!

Anne Vitte Morse
KRAMMERHUSE
Pastry cones filled with whipped cream and berries!

BATTER

2 eggs
1/3 cup sugar
3 tablespoons flour

FILLING

1 cup chilled heavy cream
1 tablespoon sugar
1 teaspoon vanilla

79

fresh or frozen raspberries or
   strawberries

Heat oven to 400°.

Beat eggs, sugar, and flour until thoroughly combined. Grease cookie sheet very well. Place 2 tablespoons of batter out to form a thin circle about 4½". Do not place more than three to four on the cookie sheet at a time; they dry out rapidly after having been baked. Bake *Krammerhuse* for 6-8 minutes, or until circles are pale gold around the edge. Quickly lift a "circle" loose from the cookie sheet using a spatula. Hold the circle in both hands, fold the two sides toward the center to form a "cone." Put the cone in a narrow glass so it keeps its shape.

Now, quickly shape the remaining baked circles. Repeat with the remaining batter. *Krammerhuse* can be baked several days in advance as long as they are kept in an airtight container. When ready to use, whip heavy cream with sugar and vanilla until stiff. Spoon whipped cream into each cone and top each with berries.

P.S. Forming these cones takes practice, especially because the "circles" are very hot. Good luck!

Velbekomme!

THE ANDERSONS

Gregg and Kay moved to Aspen from Minnesota in 1972. Gregg is the minister at the picturesque Prince of Peace Chapel. We in Aspen love to see this chapel which sits on a hill at the intersection dividing the Maroon Bells and Castle Creek valleys.

Gregg conducts two Christmas Eve services. He has one for the children complete with candles, music and singing, and a puppet show. The later service is for the adults and also has music, Christmas carol singing, and candles for decoration and effect.

The Andersons celebrate Christmas with a definite Scandinavian touch from their elaborate decorations to the traditional food they serve. Kay tells us, "The things I love most about Christmas are the wonderful smells and the special feeling of family."

Kay Anderson
SWEDISH PAN-KA-KA
(A breakfast dish)

6-10 eggs
3 cups milk
2½ teaspoons baking powder
3 strips bacon
2½ tablespoons bacon fat
1½ cups sifted flour

Beat the eggs. Add flour, baking powder, milk and bacon fat. Crumble bacon into the mixture and stir very well.

Grease a 9"×13" pan.

Preheat the oven, and be sure the oven is hot before baking.

Preheat to 500° and cook for 15 minutes.

Turn the oven down to 450° and bake for 15 minutes. Serve immediately with butter, hot syrup or honey.

Kay Anderson
SWEDISH FRUIT SOUP

large bag of mixed dried fruits (apples, apricots, prunes, pears)
extra package of dried apricots
2 large handfuls of dried prunes
½ large box white raisins
1 cinnamon stick

Put the fruit in a large kettle.

Pour water over the fruit until the fruit is covered—the water should be an extra inch above the fruit. Add the cinnamon stick. Bring to a rapid boil and cover.

Turn to low and simmer until the fruit is mushy—usually 5 hours.

An hour before done, sprinkle 2 tablespoons tapioca into the kettle and stir.

During the 5 hours, the fruit should be stirred occasionally.

Serve hot with whipped cream or ice cream. Or serve cold with yogurt or cottage cheese.

81

BIBLIOGRAPHY

The following is a list of the books we consulted in writing our book. We acknowledge both the publishers and the authors of these selected books and express our gratitude.

Coffin, Tristam Potter, *The Illustrated Book of Christmas Folklore.* New York, The Seabury Press, 1973

Hole, Christina, *Christmas And Its Customs.* New York, M. Barrows and Company, Inc., 1958

Kainen, Ruth Cole, *America's Christmas Heritage.* New York, Funk & Wagnalls, 1969

Krythe, Maymie R., *All About Christmas.* New York, Harper & Brothers, 1954

Muir, Frank, *Christmas Customs & Traditions.* New York, Taplinger Publishing Company, 1975

Rockwell, Molly (Editor), *Norman Rockwell's Christmas Book.* New York, Harry N. Abrahms, Inc., Publishers, 1977

Wernecke, Herbert H. (Editor), *Christmas Customs Around The World.* Philadelphia, The Westminster Press, 1959

RECIPE INDEX

Desserts

Dough Ornaments

Main Dishes

Salads

Spices & Preserves

Vegetables

COLOPHON

The text type is Mediaeval designed by George Trump.
Chapter headings and initial letters are Chancery Medium designed by
Hermann Zapf.
Book design and cover illustration by Curt Carpenter.